W9-DJE-617

LIVES IN THE BALANCE

SUNY Series, Urban Voices, Urban Visions
Diane DuBose Brunner and Rasidah Jaami' Muhammad, Editors

LIVES IN THE BALANCE

Youth, Poverty, and Education in Watts

Ann C. Diver-Stamnes

STATE UNIVERSITY
OF NEW YORK
PRESS

Published by
State University of New York Press, Albany

© 1995   State University of New York

Production by Susan Geraghty
Marketing by Fran Keneston

Printed in the United States of America

For information, address State University of New York Press,
State University Plaza, Albany, N.Y., 12246

Library of Congress Cataloging-in-Publication Data

Diver-Stamnes, Ann.
    Lives in the balance : youth, poverty, and education in Watts /
Ann C. Diver-Stamnes.
        p.   cm.—(SUNY series, urban voices, urban visions)
    Includes bibliographical references and index.
    ISBN 0–7914–2667–X — ISBN 0–7914–2668–8 (pbk.)
    1. Poor children—Education (Secondary)—Social aspects-
-California—Los Angeles—Case studies. 2. Education, Urban-
-California—Los Angeles—Case studies. 3. Watts (Los Angeles,
Calif.)—Social conditons. I. Title. II. Series.
LC4093.L7D58   1995
371.96'7'0979494—dc20   94-46295
                                                                  CIP

10 9 8 7 6 5 4 3 2 1

To my parents
Ardell Cecile Diver
and
Milton A. Diver
with my profound love
and gratitude

. . . Watts bleeds
dripping from carcasses of dreams:
Where despair
is old people
sitting on torn patio sofas
with empty eyes
and children running down alleys
with big sticks.

Watts bleeds
on vacant lots
and burned-out buildings—
temples desolated by a people's rage.

Where fear is a deep river.
Where hate is an overgrown weed . . .

(Reprinted by permission)
from "Watts Bleeds" by Luis J. Rodriguez
in *The Concrete River* (Willimantic, CT:
Curbstone Press, 1991).

CONTENTS

ACKNOWLEDGMENTS

With gratitude and great affection, I would like to acknowledge my students at the inner-city high school which is the focus of this book, as well as those colleagues of mine in Watts who were devoted to the education and empowerment of their students.

This book would not be complete without acknowledging my mentor and dear friend, Dr. R. Murray Thomas, professor emeritus, University of California at Santa Barbara, who taught me about the tenacity needed for scholarship and good writing.

This book is dedicated to my parents, Milt and Dell Diver, for many reasons far too numerous to describe here, foremost of which are their lifelong gifts of constant love and support.

Finally, I want to express my thanks and love to my husband, Stephen Paul Stamnes, who, with tremendous patience and meticulous care, read every word of each revised version of the manuscript for this book over the four years it has been in progress. His comments and insights permeate every chapter.

INTRODUCTION

A TEACHER'S PERSPECTIVE

Poverty is often easy to ignore—unless you are living in it. Communities in poverty, like Watts in South-Central Los Angeles, exist throughout the United States, and it is a relatively simple task to avoid them. In Los Angeles, one must simply stay on the freeway to be whisked by, further north or south, away from the disturbing images of the people whose lives are lived from day to day in the inner city.

My interest in poverty and its effects on people's lives, particularly the lives of young people, intensified when I began to teach high school in Watts while working on my dissertation for a doctorate in educational psychology. My doctoral research focused on ways to help high school students turn academic failure into success.[1] When it came time to collect the data for my dissertation, I chose a high school in the middle of government housing projects in the Watts community, a school plagued by academic failure, high absence and attrition rates, low test scores, poor basic skills, and a sagging self-image. Since my work was in academic success and failure, it seemed a stringent test of my theory to conduct the research at that particular school, a school I will call Medgar High School. I will be using pseudonyms for both the school and the people I discuss in this book as a way of preserving their anonymity.

Prior to teaching in Watts, I had taught at a suburban high school in southern California and a rural high school in southern Oregon. Nothing in my teaching experience could have prepared me for teaching at Medgar High, for the ingenuousness of the students, their lack of basic skills, and the tragedy that was the daily fare in so many of their lives. While I despaired at their general lack of reading and writing skills, I delighted in the amazing courage, altruism, and sensitivity that many of them exhibited.

Toward the end of my first year at Medgar High, I received my doctorate. At my graduation, I listened with a mixture of interest

1

and awe to the roll call of universities which were the destinations of the other graduates who were slated to assume their new professorial roles. My destination was already well known to me: I was returning to Watts to continue teaching high school. I returned for several reasons. First and foremost, I returned for "my kids", the students whose lives in one year had so profoundly touched and changed mine. I had begun work at Medgar High as an English teacher, but during my second semester, I designed and implemented two programs—Peer Counseling and the Future Teacher Program—which would, by the beginning of my second year at Medgar High, entirely consume my teaching and non-teaching time at the school. Consequently, at the end of that first year, I was flushed with a sense of accomplishment and eager to return and improve what my students and I had begun.

Further, I returned to Watts because I felt I needed to continue what I considered to be my apprenticeship prior to applying for a position at a university. If I were to become a teacher of prospective teachers, I felt I had to become the best classroom teacher I could be, and I wanted to be tested and forged in as challenging and meaningful a teaching environment as possible; Medgar High fit that description. Finally, I returned out of a need to continue answering pressing questions that seemed to multiply exponentially the longer I remained at Medgar High, questions about poverty and its effects on the lives of young people. This became a compelling need during and after that first year in Watts because the time I spent with my students and with community members had put faces in place of the statistics on poverty I could recite by rote. I became committed to gaining understanding and to writing about what I learned.

Affixing Blame versus Analyzing Causes

Just to say the name Watts evokes a reaction in many people, especially those who lived at the time of the civil unrest in Watts in 1965. Consequently, teaching in Watts over the years put me in touch with many people's opinions and perceptions about poverty in this country, its causes, and its effects on people's lives. The thinking on these subjects was widely divergent, often with little area of agreement. "Aren't the poor somehow responsible for their own condition?" some asked. Indeed, these ideas of affixing responsibility for poverty on the poor and of viewing the poor as attracting the problems that besiege their communities seem to have become accepted explanations within some factions of the dominant culture.

We live in a society in which individual acquisition and profit are valued over the needs of members of society at large. A basic premise of this society is that individuals can succeed given sufficient effort; in other words, a common view is that people can "make it" in the United States if they try hard enough. If they do not succeed, their failure is viewed as having been caused by lack of effort, and so those who are the least successful members of our society are blamed for the failure, a phenomenon called "blaming the victim."[2] Environmental factors such as chronic poverty, inadequate education, and lack of employment opportunities, to name a few, are not considered in this equation of success and failure.

Certain problems are viewed as being part of the exclusive purview of the poor. One person described the differences between a middle-class mother and a mother in poverty in the Bronx in this way:

> The [middle-class] woman . . . has a career and a good education; she probably has learned and read about parenting; she has much to offer her newborn whereas the baby in the Bronx will perhaps be born prematurely, will need state assistance, and may even become one more prison statistic or die young. These issues are pathological . . . : the neglect and abuse of children, the issue of children bearing children, the cycle of dependency on government.[3]

The perception, then, is that the problems associated with poverty are part of the pathology of the poor and that the poor are either genetically inferior or simply not trying hard enough and as a result seem incapable of changing their life situation. According to this interpretation of poverty in the United States, the long-term poor have little to offer and create the problems attendant upon their poverty.

This interpretation clashes with what I observed of people living in poverty in Watts. Certainly, such an interpretation of the lives of the poor extricates the rest of society from the responsibility of having to analyze causation and modify inequities. Is it the people themselves who are the problem or the social structures within which they are forced to interact? Some view those living in poverty as being poor by choice, whereas others hold the view that they are poor because of institutionalized inequities within the society and economic system which determine who will be at risk.[4] Since determination of "blame" seems necessary prior to society deciding upon the merit of offering assistance, this question is rigorously pursued.

The issue of assigning blame has been a centerpiece in politics and policy-making. Former vice-president Dan Quayle cited the causal factor of the civil unrest in South-Central Los Angeles in April, 1992, as being a poverty of values of the people involved. Thus, it was not the impoverished conditions of the inner cities in the United States created by years of neglect and discrimination which spawned the unrest but the people themselves who were flawed and who were lacking in values. The Bush administration, like the Reagan administration before it, avoided focusing serious attention on the problems of people living in poverty in the United States. To compound the problem, the voices of the poor are muted by their lack of political power. Politicians, who may hear best those who contribute most, often ignore the poor who lack a potent lobby to fight for them.

Thus, the relatively mute constituency of the poor has little success in communicating its needs to politicians who often find it easier to dwell on the symptoms of the problems, such as unemployed or underemployed workers, slumlike housing conditions, or people living in abject poverty, rather than the problems themselves, thus obviating the need to uncover the real causes.[5] Poor people then become the problem, rather than the inequities of the socioeconomic system. Michael Parenti compares this to being "a little like blaming the corpse for the murder."[6] Perhaps a more efficacious approach would be to determine the true underlying causes of such problems as poverty and despair and to begin upon a course of problem solving. When the toll on the nation in terms of human and financial resources is considered, the question of blame becomes irrelevant.

My experiences at Medgar High School provided me with much food for thought and propelled me toward an analysis of the causes of poverty in Watts and other inner-city communities and of the effects of that poverty, particulary on young people. I wanted to try to understand how exogenous social factors had affected the behavior and the lives of the people I met in the community. It became clear to me over time that many people, including policy makers, have an incorrect image and a flawed understanding of the realities of the lives of people in poverty. It was because of this imperfect understanding of their plight that my students asked me to promise to write this book, saying, "Tell people how it really is here. Make them understand." Beyond any modest hopes that this book may clarify these issues for those who read it, it represents the fulfillment of a promise to my students to give witness, to provide them with a voice.

A Guide to the Book

The first five chapters of the book are arranged around issues cited by those who blame the poor for their own plight as evidence of their ultimate responsibility for the state of their lives: academic failure, dysfunctional families (by dominant culture standards), adolescent maternity, child abuse, substance abuse, and gang affiliation. Throughout the book, current research is combined with anecdotal experiences in an attempt to create a clearer picture of the lives of people who live in poverty in Watts and some of the factors which perpetuate their poverty.

Chapter 1 explores academic achievement in Watts and other inner-city communities, including the reasons for the high attrition rate at Medgar High School and specific factors in public education which help to push these students out of school. For those students who do graduate from Medgar High School, their first exposure to a university can be fraught with difficulty, from the culturally biased testing they must undergo in order to enter a university through the application process, to the financial aid forms and the often foreign environment of the university itself. Chapter 1 further provides an explanation of the obstacles students from inner-city schools like Medgar High must overcome to succeed once they enter the university.

The family is the subject of Chapter 2. Adolescent maternity is a fairly commonplace and accepted occurrence at Medgar High School. Indeed, the school has an Infant Care Center attended by students' children. This chapter identifies the reasons for and the effects of the high rate of female headship of households and of out-of-wedlock maternity in Watts. Young fathers are seldom active parents in these households, and the reasons for this passive paternity are analyzed. Inner-city families often have a limited financial resource base, which causes them to create new methods for dealing with such issues as child care. "Generational blurring," one result of the utilization of multigenerational caretakers, is explored, as are issues such as the effects of adolescent maternity on the subfamily, reasons for the feminization of poverty, and causes of the increasing numbers of women and children living in poverty in Watts and other inner-city communities.

Child abuse is commonly thought to be a problem of particularly high incidence in inner-city communities, although the issue may be tied more accurately to a higher likelihood of reporting within the public health sector than within the private one. In the final section of Chapter 2, child abuse is defined and its causal factors explored, with particular focus on family-related stressors inherent in life in Watts and other poor inner-city communities.

Gang activity has spread beyond the inner city in Los Angeles into surrounding communities, reaching out into the suburbs. Gang members, in their adopted styles of dress and behavior, are easily recognizable and often strike a chord of fear in people. The view of gang members as "bad kids" is far too simplistic; Chapter 3 explores the reasons, both societal and personal, that young people like those I knew in Watts join gangs and the effects of gang affiliation on their lives.

Substance abuse, the subject of Chapter 4, was a persistent issue in my students' lives. Few of them escaped having a family member or close friend who had moved beyond use into abuse of alcohol or other drugs. In addition, peer pressure to use these substances could be quite intense, and some students succumbed to this pressure. Their reasons for substance abuse and its effects on their lives and the lives of those close to them are explored in this chapter.

Living in Watts can be a stressful experience. My students suffered from the tremendous strain of living in an environment where violence and death occurred often and without warning. Prime examples of this kind of trauma are the drive-by shootings in which innocent children, at play on their porches or in their yards, are the unintended victims of violence. Teachers at Medgar High also experienced stress as they attempted to help their students overcome the difficulties of their lives and to achieve academic success. They taught in a community where the potential for danger was high and in a school environment that was not conducive to learning. Chapter 5 explores the effects of living conditions and other stressors in Watts on the young people who live within the community and on the teachers who work with them.

Chapter 6 is an addendum. While I was working on one of the later drafts of this book, rewriting the chapter in which I discuss the lack of social change in Watts since the so-called Watts riots in 1965, South-Central Los Angeles burst into flames once again. Although I had been predicting for many years a recurrence of the violence and unrest of the 1960s, the magnitude of the loss of lives and destruction of property stunned and deeply grieved me. This book would not be complete without an examination of the current situation, the factors that led to the violence, and a reexamination of where we as a society can go from here.

Chapter 7, the final chapter, offers suggestions for change that impinge upon each area discussed in the previous chapters. As was vividly demonstrated during the 1992 civil unrest in South-Central Los Angeles, time is running out. At the heart of communities like Watts is a cancer of chronic poverty, hopelessness, and despair. Freeways can be raised so that as commuters drive by they do not have to meet the eyes of the poor but simply gaze down upon their rooftops. The "haves" can attempt to ignore those who have little or nothing at all. However, disease does not spontaneously disappear, and the cancer of hopelessness in inner cities in the United States can only be combatted by an infusion of real hope manifested in a societal commitment to meaningful and profound social change. A price is paid for delaying treatment. Poverty cannot be wished away or ignored out of existence, and the poor in Watts and other inner-city communities will continue to suffer amid myriad difficulties until the nation discovers the imagination to formulate solutions for our social problems and the vision and commitment to set those solutions into motion.

CHAPTER 1

Academic Achievement

Academic achievement in Watts is a volatile topic, volatile because inner-city students all too often receive an inadequate education, suffering from what I call academic poverty. This problem is one of long standing. After reading Herbert Kohl's *36 Children*,[1] a student in the teacher preparation program in which I now teach remarked to me how wonderful it was that the book was still current in that it continued to reflect inner-city and ghetto education after twenty-five years. No sooner had he made the remark than its pernicious implications hit him: inner-city education was too often a travesty in 1967 and continues in many cases to be a travesty today.

This chapter focuses on academic achievement in Watts, the reasons for students' academic successes and failures, and the educational opportunities for inner-city youth beyond high school.

HIGH SCHOOL

By the year 2025, minorities are expected to make up nearly 40 percent of the eighteen- to twenty-four-year-old population in the United States, yet the academic preparation of African American and Latino high school students is still well below that of whites.[2] This was especially clear at Medgar High, where the attrition rate remained consistently high and achievement and SAT scores remained consistently low. The lack of academic preparation of minorities in this country gives rise to doubts as to how well the United States will be able to compete in the world market if academic preparation for all groups does not improve in quality.

Students in kindergarten through eighth grade in Watts were often passed from grade to grade without regard for the level of skills they demonstrated. Thus, a child in the second grade who was having trouble reading at grade level was passed on to the third grade and to the fourth and fifth, until eventually she wound up in a class at Medgar High. Her skills may have slightly improved; perhaps she could read at the fourth- or fifth-grade level. At the high school, she was confronted with a very different educational system, one in which she had to actually demonstrate competence and pass the courses in which she was enrolled to be able to go on to the next grade and to graduate. Such a transition from being passed along to being held accountable for attainment of skills and units was often overwhelming and confusing. I talked with students who returned to class from the counseling office expressing anger and complete bewilderment at the news that they were not actually in tenth grade, although they had attended the ninth grade at Medgar High. They did not have sufficient units to qualify as a sophomore and were still considered ninth-grade students. "I don't care what she says," they routinely fumed, "I am not a ninth grader! I'm in the tenth!" They had been passed through the system for so many years that the notion of being held accountable for attaining skills and passing classes was a foreign one. By being passed along without having to demonstrate academic competence, students were not able to make the connection between hard work and earned academic achievement. Students perceived that they indeed were competent when they were not. Because they were being advanced to the next grade each year, they assumed that they were academically successful. I had students remark to me after a year in the ninth grade, "I used to be smart before high school."

Beyond the injustice of this sudden change of the rules was the injustice these students suffered by being allowed to slip through the educational system without acquiring skills. Imagine the fear of Wally, a ninth-grade student in one of my classes, who read at the second-grade level. He was afraid that his inability to read and write would be exposed. He refused to do work because it was easier to pass off his inability as bravado. For Wally, saying "I don't want to do it" carried a very different message than saying "I can't do it." The latter would have been too damaging; the former was a good bluff.

Referral to a special reading program gave Wally little assistance and could not reverse the damage already done to his self-esteem. He felt he had no control over his environment, lived in uneasiness, and eventually left school, where the message that he was a failure had become too repetitive and overwhelming. Once out of school, he found he lacked marketable skills, and he eventually became involved in a long series of petty crimes. The question remains as to how he survived nine years of school reading and writing at the second-grade level.

Unfortunately, his case was not unique. During my first year in Watts, the combined average reading levels of the ninth-, tenth-, and twelfth-grade students enrolled in my English classes was the sixth-grade level. Many of my students' parents were illiterate; with marginal and functional illiteracy in this country claiming some 60 million adುlts,[3] this fact in itself was not surprising. Wally was one of many students at Medgar High who suffered from one or another form of academic poverty.

Educators may be less demanding of students in inner-city schools like Medgar High because they are all too aware that their students have not "had the advantages" that some of them had as children. Many of my students' parents, concerned with survival needs, did not have the funds necessary to enjoy the luxury of providing their children with books, educational games and toys, computers, music lessons, and tutors. In what may have been intended as a sensitive response to the knowledge of their students' lack of early educational opportunities, teachers often lowered their expectations of the students at Medgar High. This kind of thinking, however, has led to a real decline in academic excellence in inner-city schools[4] and to the sad and omnipresent phenomenon of students lacking even the most basic skills.

Inner-city schools often carry a standard "attrition rate" hovering around 45 percent, and Medgar High School was no exception. This means that 45 percent of the student population at the school left for one or more of many reasons. Some students were transferred to another school as a disciplinary action or a voluntary measure, such as for protection from gangs or for perceived better educational opportunities. Some were incarcerated, joined the military, or moved their residence. They may have reached majority age and voluntarily left or were asked to leave because they had not shown sufficient academic progress. Many simply "dropped out."

The picture becomes even more disturbing. Such statistics on high school attrition rates do not take into account the startling number of students who drop out prior to high school and who never appear in descriptive statistics at Medgar High and other inner-city high schools because they were never there to be counted. The education offered to so many of these inner-city students failed to interest them and to provide them some realistic projection of future use.

Students, like those at Medgar High, who are at risk for leaving school prior to completion have special characteristics in common. They may feel that what they are being taught in school has little relevance to their lives, feel detached from school, lack motivation, have low self-esteem, and have difficulty making cognitive connections among their school subjects and between what they learn in school and real life.[5] In view of this lack of motivation and self-esteem, lack of relevance of school to the "real world," and lack of a connection between the students themselves and school, it did not seem unreasonable that these students decided to leave school before graduation. School seemed a place which had nothing to offer them and with which they felt no bond.

During my first year at Medgar High, a counselor revealed her frustration with the school and the reasons for that frustration. She said that in the previous year 73 percent of the freshman class did not pass to the tenth grade. Of the tenth graders that year, 68 percent were retained. The figures for the juniors and seniors were somewhat better, but the classes had already been severely reduced by then: 39 percent of the juniors and 23 percent of the seniors were retained. This level of failure became graphic when the ninth-grade students with whom I had entered the school graduated four years later. At a ninth-grade class assembly in the beginning of that year, the students in this class nearly filled the auditorium. When their class graduated four years later, they fit on a stage seated in folding chairs.

The causes of such massive failures in education were numerous. The family was one contributing factor; family background is considered the most important determinant of educational attainment.[6] Research shows that higher family income is associated with greater likelihood of school completion,[7] which has obvious implications for schools like Medgar High serving low-income communities like Watts. Children living in a female-headed household are further at risk in terms of school participation: their odds of dropping out of school by sixteen or seventeen increase by 30 to 50 percent.[8] With so many children in Watts living in poverty in female-headed households, some of the underlying reasons for the high attrition rate at Medgar High begin to become clear. In Los Angeles Unified School District, several of the causes of students being behind grade level dealt directly with family issues, including large family size, low socioeconomic status, and female household headship.[9] These factors could be applied to many of my students' families.

Community members who had attended Medgar High during earlier decades spoke of the high value placed on education by their parents, the strong commitment in the family to academic achievement, and the abiding expectation held by their parents that their children work hard to succeed in school. The African American family structure, so strong in the 1940s, 1950s, and 1960s, underwent major changes in the 1970s and 1980s from a traditional two-parent structure to female household headship. Without the necessary structure from which to instill such values as a desire for education or achievement, the gains made earlier by African Americans in the area of education slowed to a halt.[10] The Medgar High graduates from earlier decades with whom I spoke pinpointed the family as a major cause of the changes in the student population at the high school.

Some of my students' parents, both African American and Latino, did not express a strong value for education. As a consequence, their children studied late at night or hid under their bedcovers using a flashlight to read their textbooks or do homework. These parents felt that their children's time was better spent in taking care of the house and their siblings or in getting a job outside the home. Often this had a practical application, since such active participation in child care, housekeeping, and employment was needed for survival of the family.

Research shows that parents who have abdicated the major responsibility for their children's education to the public school system will be more likely to see their offspring leave school with inadequate preparation prior to graduation.[11] Parent involvement at inner-city schools is often minimal, and this also contributed to the unchecked continuation of many of the problems at Medgar High. Parents who were not involved in their children's education in Watts cited a variety of reasons: lack of knowledge about the school's functions and their own rights to participate in their children's education, lack of understanding as to how they could be involved, fear of intruding where they may not have been wanted, embarrassment at their own lack of education, other pressing family responsibilities and obligations, and the demands of their jobs. It was difficult for some of my students' parents in Watts to be involved in their children's education in light of the tremendous obstacles they battled daily, including, for those who worked, long hours of labor that precluded the luxury of visits with their children's teachers. Those parents who did not speak English had the added burden of attempting to communicate with the largely English-speaking staff of teachers and counselors. Further, a lack of intercultural competence on the part of school personnel and faculty and an exhibition of condescension by some staff members may have inhibited rather than encouraged parental involvement. For example, staff members repeatedly joked that the way to get parents to come to school activities was to provide free food. Such an attitude could not help but be communicated to the parents, some of whom felt degraded by such perceptions. Since the parents' involvement in their children's education was essential to maintaining quality education and preventing abuses, parents needed to be welcomed at the school site and treated with respect. All too often, this did not occur.

This is not to say that all parents were equally interested in being involved in their children's academic lives. Back-to-school and open house functions were poorly attended no matter what time they were held. It was not unusual in my first two years at the school to have only a few parents come to my classroom during parent-teacher functions. The administration offered prizes to teachers who were able to bring in the largest number of parents to the school for such occasions, and some teachers would give their students rewards of extra credit points or posters or buttons if their parents were in attendance. Teachers were encouraged to call all of their students' parents or guardians to ask them to attend the functions, an activity that was beyond the realm of the possible for many teachers. Thus, some of the responsibility for parental attendance was transferred from the parents to the teachers, a move that caused some grumbling among the already overburdened faculty.

Toward the end of my time at Medgar High, more parents began to attend these parent-teacher functions. Some people maintained that the parent attendance was up because of the shifting demographics at the school: the increase in the Latino population was cited as the reason for the increase in parent participation. Such reasoning, of course, did not take into consideration the cultural differences between those individuals in Watts who were well established within the community and who had experienced long-term discrimination and poverty and those who were new voluntary immigrants to both the country and the community and who still viewed education as a sure method of achieving success in the United States. In short, staff members at Medgar High who put forth the viewpoint that the influx of Latinos into the school was good because the Latino families would be involved in their children's education (as opposed to a lack of involvement of African American families) seemed unaware of the racist implications of their statements and of the need for a deeper analysis of the issue, including the effects of a legacy of oppression, racism, and a lack of opportunity.

Others at the school cited the increased efforts of the administration to send out fliers and telephone messages to the community as the cause of the increased parent participation. Still others said that moving the functions to the evening rather than the daytime enabled many more parents to attend. The functions had been held during school hours because of the safety issue for teachers traveling out of the neighborhood at night.

Because many of my students' parents had not finished high school, they had few successful academic role models. These students observed people with money who often came by their wealth through illicit means rather than by completing their education. It was a common refrain with some students I knew who had trouble reading or writing or doing basic mathematical calculations that they did not need an education because they could get money through selling drugs. In a city where unemployment for minority youth runs close to 50 percent,[12] a high school diploma was no guarantee of employment. Some students saw little reason to finish their education and become involved in "legitimate" pursuits when they observed friends who had graduated in previous years struggling and often failing to find a job and support themselves.

In addition, peer pressure discouraged students from being academically successful. Some students referred to their successful peers as "school boys" and "school girls." Such terms carried a strong negative connotation. Further, some successful students were derided as "acting white." Thus, success in academic endeavors was strongly associated with behaviors typical of white students, and students who attempted to do well in school were seen as trying to act like white people. The sad counterpoint to this charge was the unspoken logic behind it: the students in Watts who held this view thought that doing well in school was not a part of the cultural repertoire of African Americans and Latinos, and so to do well was to deny their own ethnicity and heritage. Without a wealth of successful role models, students continued to hold the idea that to be academically successful meant that they must deny their cultural identity and become completely assimilated into white, mainstream culture, which was a painful forced choice.

It was not that role models did not exist in Watts; they did. A first grader at the local elementary school across the street from Medgar High told me that when he grew up he wanted to go to jail. When I asked him about his reasons, he replied that his father and older brothers were there, so he would get arrested and go to jail too. He said, "Then I'll be able to see my daddy and my brothers." To a six-year-old boy who missed the males in his family, the role models of his father and brothers were immediate, powerful, and poignant.

Older siblings served as positive role models for some children in Watts. Those adolescents involved in sibling caretaking sometimes took their responsibilities so seriously that they attended school functions in lieu of their parents and had conferences with their younger brothers' or sisters' teachers, fully adopting even these parenting roles. On open house nights and at other parent-teacher functions, I routinely reported students' progress to their slightly older brothers and sisters, aunts and uncles, or cousins, who smiled in shy pride at good reports and made mock threats to the student about continued progress.

Even in the presence of parental and familial involvement in education, inner-city schools like Medgar High contribute to the undereducation of their students by perpetuating the system of inequitable education offered to the poor in this country. This can be accounted for by a number of reasons. First, children between the ages of six and sixteen have more equal access to education than younger or older children.[13] Access to preschool and university is not equal for all individuals or groups. Although public education is available to all children, the expense of preschools and universities restricts access to them. Certainly, most families living in poverty in Watts were not able to pay for private early educational opportunities for their children. Consequently, the children arrived at the schoolhouse doors with few skills that would help to increase their learning readiness, unlike their more advantaged counterparts.

Further, the United States spends twice as much in education on children of the rich than on those of the poor,[14] so equity in terms of financing simply does not exist. Expenditures per student are not equal from state to state, district to district, or school to school within one district. As much as some politicians attempt to segregate quality education from issues of funding, the fact remains that a school that is able to spend twice as much per year per pupil as a school in a nearby poor district will be able to offer a significantly enriched environment and higher quality education.[15] The education students received at Medgar High was inferior to that received by more advantaged children at other schools around the state and even within the same district. This was a fact of life recognized by both staff and students alike.

De facto segregation results in many inner-city schools having only minority enrollment; thus, they are not reflective of the society at large. Medgar High School was an example of this. With its outdated textbooks and crumbling, dirty facilities, it operated in conditions which would not have been tolerated in other mixed or predominantly white communities. During a visit to a high school outside Watts, a colleague whispered to me that this school felt like a "real school." The differences between Medgar High and the school we were visiting, both within the same district, were strikingly obvious. The sad implications of this remark did not hit me until long after I had left Medgar High: if the school we were visiting was a "real school," then what was Medgar High in our estimation?

Inequities existed at Medgar High in the treatment of students as well. At the school site, some students were favored or promoted over others. According to R. Clark, "The way in which time, curriculum, personnel, and material resources are allocated within neighborhood schools tends to promote the development of a few children at the expense of many other children."[16] Those students who appeared able to succeed received disproportionate amounts of staff time and attention. Since the majority of students experienced serious problems and debilitating difficulties in their lives, both personally and academically, staff found themselves in the position of needing to focus their limited time and energy on those students they perceived they could "save." This amounted to a form of academic triage. As in any triage situation, those who were viewed to be beyond help were ignored in favor of those who were deemed to have a chance. The term *throwaway kid* was used to refer to an adolescent with whom it was perceived nothing could be done. The debate in working with troubled youth at the school always centered around whether school staff perceived that they could "save" them: "This kid is troubled, but he is basically a good kid, and I think we can save him. He's not a throwaway." Such discussions seemed to take on an evangelical tone, but they revolved around a very real allocation of a limited resource: staff time.

Two segments of the student body claimed attention at the school: those who were in some positive way considered special (athletic, bright, verbal, musical, artistic, charismatic, or active) and those who were consistently in trouble. These students were generally well known by staff and students alike. Those in the middle, the "unspecial," were frequently overlooked.[17] In Watts, the "unspecial" often suffered the multiple handicaps of being inner-city students, possessing weak academic skills, and lacking the personal resources to attract staff attention. Counselors at the high school complained that they spent so much of their time dealing with kids in trouble that they never knew the majority of their counselees. It brings to mind the question as to how a viable academic program can be created for students when their aspirations and abilities are unknown quantities.

Undereducation, which schools in Watts and other inner-city communities all too often offer to their students, can begin in elementary school, where students who do not respond in ways deemed consistent with the dominant culture are often ignored and placed in groups of other like students and are labeled slow learners or low achievers.[18] Ray Rist noted the beginnings of the failure of the educational system in kindergarten, where the teacher separated students into ability groups based on social-class information rather than academic ability.[19] Thus, children who spoke standard English, were middle class, and were clean and neatly dressed were placed in the high-ability group, and those who spoke Ebonics ("Black" English), were living in poverty, were dirty and sometimes smelled of urine, and were poorly dressed were placed in the low-ability group. Such tracking follows children through their academic careers and becomes a self-fulfilling prophecy.

One teacher in Rist's study called her student groups the Tigers, the Cardinals, and the Clowns, with the Clowns being considered the lowest-ability group. Rist wrote, "To call a group of students 'clowns' was more than a mere evaluation of their academic performance. It was a statement of their perceived worth as individuals."[20] Children within the high group received two to three times as much academic instruction as the others did, and whereas their assignments were academic, the assignments the "Clowns" received were nonacademic. A teacher expressed her opinion that one of her students would never do anything in life; the boy was in the second grade.

Like Rist, I have had the opportunity to observe elementary classrooms serving minority children and spent considerable time at two local elementary schools where my students worked with, tutored, and taught the children. I spoke with children in Watts in the first and second grade who hated school with good reason. Children who were labeled at five as slow or troublemakers or somehow undesirable because their clothes were dirty or their skin was darker than the other children's or their English was "non-standard" did not fathom the true reasons for their ostracism from the favored group. They did not know that they were giving social, verbal, and nonverbal cues to their teacher that automatically excluded them from the "high achievers," those who were allowed to cluster around the teacher and who received a great deal of the teacher's attention in personal, social, and academic interactions. They only perceived that they were on the fringes, were not loved and accepted. They adopted a quite logical response: they tuned out. I have observed second graders in Watts who literally turned their backs on the teacher, and, after watching the interactions between the teacher and the students, that response seemed to be entirely logical and understandable.

Some of the children I observed in kindergarten or first grade who already were labeled as troublemakers were victims of an abusive and dysfunctional home and an uninformed and at times uncaring school. Children who had been neglected, for example, came to school requiring a great deal of attention from the adults with whom they came in contact. Children who had been so-called drug babies, that is, whose mothers regularly had ingested drugs during their pregnancy, exhibited behaviors in the classroom that were often highly disruptive. Teachers rarely knew about the problems caused by fetal drug exposure or about appropriate methodologies for working with such children. The children's need for consistent individual attention was often overwhelming for teachers trying to deal with a classroom of twenty-five or thirty children. I heard teachers routinely criticize children for needing "too much attention," and it was precisely these children who were labeled, sent to the principal, asked to sit in the hall, and ultimately ostracized from the group. If teachers are not aware of the dilemmas and daily lives of the population of students they are teaching, then it is quite likely that they will exhibit insensitivity and a lack of understanding in their interactions with those children. In essence, we have to teach the students as they come to us, and in the case of the students in Watts, they often came to us in tremendous need.

Within one first-grade bilingual classroom in Watts, I observed three African American boys sitting at a table by themselves while the teacher, the aide, and one of my high school students worked with the three other groups. During the times I observed the class, all instruction took place in Spanish, which these three children did not speak. They were clearly bored, and the only interaction they had with the teacher while I was in the room was one in which she stood over them and yelled (in English) for them to be quiet. It seems clear that, as Rist wrote, "To put it more bluntly, the teachers themselves contributed significantly to the creation of the 'slow learners' within their classrooms."[21] However, simply pointing to the teachers' role does not get to the root of the problem.

Why were some teachers in Watts using such obviously counterproductive and harmful methodologies? Many of them were never taught about the special needs of the particular population of children they ended up teaching. Responsibility for this inadequate preparation rests with the teacher preparation programs for their initial lack of training and with the districts for their lack of viable, practical in-service training. The districts may perhaps be the best place for offering teachers specific teaching methodologies to use with a particular population, leaving the teacher preparation programs to utilize a broad approach.

When I arrived at Medgar High, I was interested to learn that all "new teachers" were to be involved in a program designed to offer them support as they began their teaching careers at the school. I assumed that such intervention would take the form of educating those of us who were new to inner-city education about the special needs of our student population and about the Watts community. This was not the case. Teachers who were new to the profession, those who were teaching on an emergency credential and who had no formal teacher training, and experienced teachers who were new to the school were lumped under the heading *new teacher*. The training took the format of a series of lectures on how to take role, how to discipline, how to write a lesson plan, and how to deal with issues such as students chewing gum in class. A colleague and I, both experienced teachers who had held teaching credentials for a number of years, found this approach insulting and unhelpful. After confronting the coordinator with our situation and finding she had no intention of dealing with the issues of teaching at an inner-city high school, we simply stopped attending these "required" sessions. This is a classic example of how the implementation of what amounted to a good idea, that of orienting teachers to working in the inner city, in essence widely missed its mark and indeed alienated those who participated in it.

Students who were taught by teachers who were insensitive to the realities of their daily lives changed over time. The evolution of these young people from turned-off second grader to high school "dropout" was not difficult to fathom. Many students who were excluded from the educational process as children never attained the skills necessary to be able to succeed in school. A kindergartner I repeatedly observed sitting in the principal's office at the elementary school ended up spending many hours in the office through first, second, and third grade. It was painful to watch the hope drain out of him over the years. He entered the school troubled; however, the school created and labeled the "troublemaker." The only way he received attention was by acting out, and he became quite skillful at it. He lived up to the level of his teachers' expectations as students tend to do, and since they had only expectations for poor performance, he performed poorly. By the time he was in the third grade, he wore his label as troublemaker with pride. It was far too easy to see him as a future hall walker at the high school in another six or seven years, wandering through the corridors and disrupting classes, if he did not drop out of school before then.

Constant exposure to failure eventually fostered either anger or apathy. Students ultimately opted out of the system because they could not win within it, and to lose constantly was far too self-damaging. The tenth grader who decided to leave the school had already invested nine-plus years of his life in what he perceived to be a losing proposition. Some educators argue that these highly at-risk students do not have the choice of "opting out" or dropping out and prefer the term *push out* to transfer responsibility for failure to the educational system rather than the students. In light of the systemic failure we experienced at Medgar High, this transfer of responsibility seems appropriate.

In such a context, the students and sometimes young community members in Watts who roamed the halls of the high school and created havoc with students and teachers alike became comprehensible. They felt rage at having been cheated, at finding themselves excluded because of their lack of skills from what occurred inside the classroom. Their exclusion became literal when they stopped going to classes and began to "hang" in the halls and the stairwells, on the field, or on the quad. They vented their rage against teachers, the buildings, and successful students. As is so often the case in education, our response to these students was reactive rather than proactive: we simply locked our classroom doors.

Students who are involved in active rebellion may participate in an "illicit curriculum" which includes a variety of ways of avoiding the "legitimate" curriculum of the school without actually dropping out.[22] Such on-campus acts as using alcohol or other drugs; being involved in illegal activities such as graffiti, theft, and assault; and urinating and defecating in the stairwell made up the "illicit" curriculum at Medgar High. These students were highly skillful in avoiding security guards, "ditching" (skipping or cutting class), climbing the fences to leave school, and bluffing their way past the security guard at the front door in order to leave campus.

Teachers who had graduated from the school some years before spoke of the changes in the student population since they had attended: observable declines in respect for authority, academic excellence, and interest in education. The older adult members of the Site Improvement Council at the school spoke of the years when they were students at Medgar High and described a place utterly removed from the school it had become. Perhaps the future had seemed to hold out more to these earlier graduates. In the 1980s and the early 1990s, the few of my students in Watts who were able to find work did so at fast-food restaurants working for minimum wage, and their prospects upon completion of high school were no brighter. When students announced that they had landed a job, a common question was "Are you working for the colonel or the clown?" This was in reference to working at Kentucky Fried Chicken or McDonald's fast-food outlets, the extent of opportunity for many of the young people I knew in Watts. Thus, students often expressed a hopelessness about their future prospects that was not conducive to motivating them to complete their education. They asked, "What's the point?"

Although minority graduation rates are increasing, they are still below those of whites.[23] Some Medgar High students did graduate, of course, in a tremendously emotional celebration of having beaten the odds. It was impossible to sit through a graduation celebration at the high school without being moved. Parents seated around me at the last graduation ceremony I attended leaned forward to pat my shoulders when they saw the tears in my eyes as I watched my students walk up to receive their diplomas. "You have a right to be proud," they whispered to me.

These young graduates, so proud and exultant, were being sent out into the world, and yet many were not equipped to compete. Their attendance at an all-minority inner-city high school, their cultural encapsulation, their lack of financial resources, and their flawed and inadequate education were the handicaps they carried with them as they accepted their diplomas. It was the knowledge of these handicaps and of the students' struggle to overcome them that gave the graduation ceremonies their profound poignancy. It was also the knowledge of all they had to overcome in order to march in graduation: the gangs avoided, the drugs not ingested, the pregnancies thwarted, the poverty endured, the abuses survived.

For some of these students, this was a high point in their lives, and they felt that it was unlikely that it would ever be matched again. Their senior year represented the peak in their social interactions and academic achievement. Their prom pictures possessed added meaning because of this. They graduated, and the fortunate ones went on to vocational school, to college, or to work. Some married and became pregnant. Some were pregnant as they walked up to accept their diplomas.

There was another reason for tears at graduation ceremonies at Medgar High: grief at the knowledge of how many we lost. Look at the graduating class of a typical inner-city high school and realize that up to three-quarters of the original class members are not present. This is beyond failure; it is a travesty.

EDUCATION AFTER HIGH SCHOOL

For some students in Watts, graduation from high school marked the end of their academic careers; they donned cap and gown but once. It was for this reason that, on the days before graduation when caps and gowns already had been distributed, students strode purposefully down the street in full regalia. These were moments to be savored. Community members honked and called out their congratulations as these students walked briskly by the government housing projects flanking the high school.

For most high school students, entrance into college is not an easy feat, and this was particularly true of Medgar High School students. The application process was often intimidating. Further, research shows that social class is a dominant factor in determining the accessibility of higher education and the subsequent perseverance and success of students,[24] and students from Medgar High, who left high school at a distinct disadvantage, found it difficult to enter into colleges and universities and even more difficult to remain there once they arrived. Fewer than one in five college-age minorities are enrolled in college.[25] Part of my job as a teacher at Medgar High was to introduce college as a possible life option; for so many of my students, it had never even been considered.

College entrance requirements include providing the college or university with scores on standardized entrance examinations and transcripts which also show results of previous standardized tests administered at school. Medgar High ranked at the bottom of schools in Los Angeles County in California Assessment Program (CAP) test scores in math and reading. The school scored 1 in both reading and math on a scale of a low of 1 to a high of 99 with a medial rank of 50.[26] Even though many tests are thought to be culturally biased, covering, as they do, material which was often not a part of the life experience of students from the inner city, they exerted a strong influence on the life chances of students from Medgar High. Many children in Watts experienced cultural encapsulation and socioeconomic disadvantages which in some cases had spanned generations. They were tested with instruments based on conformity with a dominant-culture model of appraisal. Thus, these were really tests of assimilation into the culture, not, as they were touted to be, tests of intelligence or achievement. It did not surprise me that my students did not do well on them.

Many of these students were not enrolled in a college preparatory sequence of courses in high school (or, as was sometimes said, "tracked into college prep"), and this may have caused them to score lower on the Scholastic Aptitude Test (SAT). The SAT is used as a predictor of college performance and is based on academic preparedness,[27] and students who have not received adequate preparation are likely to produce lower scores; Medgar High students went into the tests at a distinct disadvantage. They often did not have access to intensive SAT preparatory courses, as did many of their more fortunate peers. Although such courses are not known to have a significant effect on test scores,[28] they can help to reduce or alleviate test anxiety caused by lack of familiarity with the testing process. In all the time I was teaching in Watts, not one of my seniors reported to me a combined SAT test score above 900, and most were in the 600 to 800 range. Although some educators may see this as a failure of minorities, it is rather a failure of the educational system[29] to provide adequate, equitable education.

If they attend college, minority students are more likely to go to a community college than to a four-year institution. Students in Watts followed this trend, and the logic behind their decision was sound. They realized that they had not been well prepared and that competition with students who were better prepared would be stiff. They talked about going to a community college as a way of "getting used to college" prior to going on to a four-year institution. It constituted, then, a transition step from high school to a university, often a needed one. Fewer minority students, however, are transferring to four-year institutions,[30] which means that for some of my students the transition from community college to a four-year university never occurred. The quality of their transfer degree was a strong factor in enrollment at a four-year institution, and they needed wise counseling early in their academic careers so that they took courses which would be counted in the transfer. Without such counseling, they lost credits, which functioned as a disincentive to matriculate. Medgar High graduates who did not know how to function within the system found themselves in the predicament of attempting to transfer and discovering that they had not taken the required courses or had taken courses that would not be accepted at the university to which they applied.

Students from Medgar High who did progress to college were often unable to graduate. Research shows that minorities consistently fall through the cracks of the educational system and are unable to finish high school, college, and graduate school much more often than their nonminority counterparts.[31] Medgar High graduates left college for both academic and nonacademic reasons. They often arrived at college in need of remediation; that is, their skills were not as high as those of their more advantaged peers, so they needed extra assistance in the form of remedial coursework and tutoring. Such courses are lacking at many colleges and universities, and faculty resistance to teaching remedial courses appears to be a contributing factor.[32] University professors, who are considered to be experts in their disciplines but are not necessarily experts in teaching methodology, often know little or nothing about how to teach students with special needs; some feel that such students do not belong at the university. It is essential that "we work with what we've got"[33] at universities rather than bicker over which grade level failed students with poor skills who are entering universities. Thus, the issue is not that students should have acquired these skills prior to entering the university or that the university is not the place to deal with students in need of "remediation." The issue quite plainly revolves around a simple credo in education that we teach the students as they come to us, not as we envision they should be.

Although clearly effective remediation and ongoing counseling for students like those from Medgar High are needed to maximize retention, the funding for such programs is difficult to obtain,[34] especially in a time of extreme budget cuts at all state universities in California. Some faculty see little need to expend any of the scarce resources on maximizing retention when classes are already filled to overflowing. Students from Watts and other inner-city high schools are the first to leave school in these times of dwindling human services and financial aid. Because their education has been inferior and their familiarity with university protocol is scant, they are often unable to get the extra assistance they need to be successful at the university, and they leave.

Medgar High School students said that they felt they were in an alien world when they went to college, and in many senses they were. Their previous academic experiences took place in a segregated environment where whites were rarely present in the student population. They lived in a socioeconomically impoverished community. At college, especially for those who lived on campus, they suddenly found themselves in the minority. They were confronted with students who came from more affluent families. Research shows that minority students often do not become assimilated into the dominant culture at the college or university, maintaining an allegiance to peer groups of like minorities,[35] and this was true of the students I knew from Watts. This kind of allegiance inhibited interaction among the various ethnic and racial groups on campus and prevented students from being able to establish a real connection or bond with the institution, which functioned as a deterrent to achieving a degree. The rising racism on college campuses only served to further weaken the already tenuous connection between the institution and these Medgar High graduates.

One student from Watts, Mari, who attended a University of California campus and lived in a dormitory, related to me that she had no white female friends, a few white male friends, and many African American and Latino friends. She said the white female students were cordial but not friendly. "They say hi in the bathroom in the morning, but we never do anything together socially. They stick to themselves," she said. Apparently, the pressure on campus was also strong among minority students to maintain friendships only with other minority students, and Mari found herself defending her attempts to befriend people of other races and ethnicities, something she was anxious to do because of her years of education in Watts in de facto segregated schools. When I first met Mari, she later revealed to me, she did not like whites. During her ninth- and tenth-grade years, we spent much time talking as she struggled and came to terms with her own prejudices, and this became an area of abiding interest for her. For Mari, going to the university was a chance to interact with a diverse population of people with whom she had previously had little contact and to explore her own issues of racism, prejudice, stereotypes, and oppression.

Mari's African American and Latino friends at the university asked her why she was "talking to that white boy" or "listening to that white music." Such comments invariably sparked heated arguments that clearly defined the ethnic and racial barriers that these students felt they should honor. Mari explicitly wanted to make friends with students from the dominant culture. After two years of attending the university, she reported that she had finally met one white student, a woman, with whom she felt she was cultivating a friendship. All of her other friends and her roommates were Latino and African American, and this was a source of frustration to her.

Most Medgar High graduates found that the quality of their precollege education was inadequate, and their lack of preparation caused some of them such difficulty that they decided to leave their college or university. As one graduate complained to me when she returned to the high school for a visit, "I didn't even know what an atom was! My roommate had to tell me. I'd never used a computer! It was humiliating. I felt so stupid. We never learned these things here so the other students are miles ahead of us. I am always trying to catch up on what I didn't learn in high school just so that I can understand what is being taught in college."

Many Medgar High graduates had difficulty securing sufficient financial aid to attend college. Such problems are common, especially at those institutions which have a large default rate on student loans and whose federal funds are being cut.[36] The process of filling out the financial aid application forms required a certain amount of savvy and experience. My students were first-generation college students; consequently, they did not have parents who had gone to college on whom they could rely for help in the lengthy application process or in the cultivation of expectations of university life. Some concerned teachers and staff at the high school assisted them. Medgar High students who crossed the threshold onto a university campus represented the tremendous combined effort of the students themselves, family, faculty, and staff.

Beyond the academic sphere, life itself caused interruptions in their academic careers. Students found, for example, that they were expecting a child or experienced urgent family problems. Some young women from tradition-bound microcultures had to fight a constant battle with their families and their boyfriends over their quest for higher education, which was viewed as unnecessary for a woman. Such battles often sapped their energy, their confidence, and their time.

My students provided a compelling picture of their lives in college. One student's mother left the state shortly before the end of her freshman year. The student lived with a friend of her mother's until it became clear that she was no longer welcome. At that point, she would have become homeless but for a community activist who had set up a house as a sort of dormitory for young women going to school and working who either had dysfunctional home situations or who had nowhere to go. Through all of this turmoil and at last report, she was still in college.

Another student was accepted into a prestigious California university. Once there, he was confronted with academic challenges beyond any he had imagined, although a few teachers had worked hard to try to prepare him for the challenges he would surely meet. His letters from the university were filled with wonder at all the accomplishments of his classmates, accomplishments he had not confronted in his peers before. One student could sit down and play classical music on the piano from memory. Another had been in journalism in high school and had been hired by a local paper to write for them part-time. Another was an accomplished photographer, and another had more CDs (compact discs) than he had ever seen anywhere. All of his classmates had personal computers. He wrote that he knew it would be difficult but that he was sure he could get by with his old manual typewriter. He had no experience with computers and lacked the funds to buy one.

During the first semester, this student left the university. His stated reason was that his mother was ill and needed him at home because all the other children were gone. (His father had left the family before he was born.) A classmate of his who was attending the same university said the reason he left was that he was failing all of his classes. He returned to Los Angeles and went to work in an office, commuting two hours each way by bus every day. He continued to dream of all that he could do in his life and continued to be haunted by the label given to him in his senior year of high school: most likely to succeed. Upon hearing of his return to Watts, I wondered how he could have competed with an inferior education, inadequate materials, constant worry about his mother's health, limited financial resources, little assistance, and no idea of what he needed to do to be able to succeed in such a foreign environment. He spoke of feeling like he was in another country while at the university, and in effect he was, for he had come from the inner city, the "other America" of extreme poverty,[37] a world away from the life of relative privilege and ease from which so many of his classmates derived.

Some of the students I knew were able to succeed in college. Some were gifted or courageous or tenacious or had whatever combination of the three equals success. It was never easy, however. These were students who had little experience with the bureaucracy that universities can be. Even after they left for college, I continued to hear from them as they asked me for advice: "I'm behind in my Bio. class. What do I do?" "My financial aid didn't come through. What should I do?"

Changes in university priorities could help to ease the transition for inner-city students. Recruitment is only one way to increase minority enrollment, and students continue to need support and assistance after they declare their intention to attend a particular institution. Medgar High students were often baffled by the academic maze a university can be. They needed ongoing assistance to help guide them through the process and to ease them into university life. Follow-up mentoring and programs addressing retention were as important as recruitment.

Much of my time in the first semester of each school year in Watts was spent helping my seniors fill out applications for college admission, calling schools to ask for information or status reports on their applications, filling out financial aid applications, helping them to write and type essays, and even doing their families' taxes so they could complete the financial aid forms. They did not know how to deal with the mountains of paperwork and deadlines involved in getting into college. Once at the college or university, they continued to need an enlightened guide as they confronted the new bureaucracy of their school, and their peers often helped to facilitate this transition in the absence of staff assistance or a faculty mentor.

Medgar High students who finished twelve years of school, passed their competency tests, received their diplomas, and entered college showed that it could happen, even though the process was arduous and often painful, filled with the pitfalls of a foreign culture, a sense of personal inadequacy, new and bewildering rules, and the responsibility for their own success and failure. The transition to the university could have been so much easier on them if they had had a mentor at that level as some of them had at the high school, someone who understood firsthand the environment from which they came, the education they received and its failings, their naivete of bureaucracies, their confusion at suddenly being thrown into a culturally diverse environment, and their self-doubt as they compared themselves to their classmates. Such one-on-one interaction of minority students with a skilled and caring mentor could do much to reduce the attrition rate of minorities at the college level. In particular, students from Medgar High and other inner-city high schools have come so far and overcome so much once they arrive at the gates of the university that it is tragic to allow them to turn back without Herculean efforts on the part of the institution to retain them.

CHAPTER 2

Families in Watts

A fourteen-year-old girl tells her teacher that she has been absent from school for the past week because her baby boy is ill, and, since the infant care center on campus will not accept students' children when they are sick, she had to stay home with him. A fifteen-year-old girl is absent from school for a month because she was left at home to take care of her brothers and sisters while her mother returned to her country of birth to care for a dying parent. To those who have never worked with adolescents in the inner city, it may be difficult to imagine these young people in their roles as parents and primary caregivers of younger siblings. However, such roles were common to young people in Watts, causing inevitable conflict between family and education. In such a loaded conflict, the long-term benefits of education are often passed over for the immediate needs or demands of the family.[1] As in other inner-city communities, institutional support systems were all too often lacking in Watts, and so the family, both primary and extended, helped to fill in the gaps, especially in terms of child care.

The dynamics of families living in Watts often reflected the realities of living in or near poverty. The cycle of early pregnancy, lack of education, and unemployment that was so tragically obvious in Watts is just one manifestation of the cold statistics compiled by the U.S. Bureau of the Census: women and children increasingly make up the ranks of the poor. In Watts, families, often headed by women, bear the brunt of poverty, attempting to maintain a stable family life at great cost and against seemingly insurmountable odds. This chapter will discuss issues confronting youth and their families in Watts, including adolescent maternity, multigenerational caregivers, female household headship and its causes and effects, women and children in poverty, "generational blurring," which occurs when children are raised by older siblings or grandparents, and families in crisis.

ADOLESCENT MATERNITY

The scene became a familiar one to me. A young woman, the friend of one of my students, came to my classroom door, asking to speak with me. She began with a small problem, something simple, speaking in such a distracted fashion that I quickly understood that what she was saying was not the real reason for her visit. Eventually, she ducked her head, averting her eyes from mine, and talked about how difficult it was to broach the real subject because she was embarrassed. I knew then the purpose of her visit to my office: she thought she was pregnant. I hauled out the well-thumbed calendar I used for such purposes, and together we figured out the date of her last menstrual period and the number of days her period was now late. We discussed various symptoms of pregnancy to see if she was experiencing any of them. We talked about her mother, with whom she lived, her boyfriend, and her feelings about a possible pregnancy. She asked me to help her tell her mother if she was indeed pregnant. We ended by discussing the need for a pregnancy test and medical care and the locations of the nearest women's clinics. This conversation was repeated with astounding frequency with my students and their friends, many of whom would turn up at my classroom door asking if I would explain to them "the calendar thing."

Babies seemed omnipresent at Medgar High School. In my journal from my first year in Watts, I wrote, "I seem to be becoming inured to all that happens around me here: drugs, rape, beatings, incest, poverty, pregnancy, and babies, babies, babies . . . " Some young mothers were able to bring their children to school and leave them at the on-campus infant care center. Little ones often visited my classes with their parents, my students. It was not uncommon for me to teach classes while entertaining a student's toddler whose child care had fallen through for the day. It seemed ironic to me that school policy expressly forbade students from bringing their children or siblings to class: this policy was yet another example of how we failed to confront the realities of our students' lives and to encourage them in their struggle to meld school and family. In my classroom, we disregarded the policy. We always had crayons, construction paper, and blunt scissors on hand. Because so many of my students functioned as caregivers of siblings, their own children, or the children of extended family members, they were entirely at ease with children, adept at caring for them, and completely natural in their interactions with them.

In Watts, as in other inner-city communities, the picture was grim. One-fourth of the young women at Medgar High had babies each year, and approximately 80 percent of the African American children in Watts are born to unmarried mothers.[2] Only one of the young mothers in my classes was married at the time of her child's birth. The traditional two-parent or nuclear family, common within the African American community in the United States until World War II, has now become the exception. This shift from two-parent families to female-headed households, so evident in Watts, was caused by such factors as increases in divorce and out-of-wedlock births and decreases in the marriage rate.[3]

African Americans and Latinos composed the two primary ethnicities in the Watts community, and shifts were occurring within Latino as well as African American households. Poverty has remained steady and high for all types of families in the Latino community. Throughout the country, the increase has not been in the rate of poverty for these families but in the numbers of families living in poverty and, in particular, the startling 95 percent increase between 1974 and 1984 in the number of Spanish-origin female-headed households.[4] As with all ethnicities, Latino households headed by women experienced the highest rate of poverty.

Thus, in ever-increasing numbers women in Watts were functioning as heads of households and were living in poverty. Indeed, more families of women and children were poor in this country in the 1980s than at any time in its history as the result of such factors as divorce, single parenthood, unemployment and low wages, inadequate child support awards, nonpayment of child support, and high fertility.[5] The situation seemed chronically bleak in the inner cities, where approximately 50 percent of female-headed families were poor. Their poverty was greater and of longer duration than that of other groups. Certainly, such issues as depth and duration of poverty were of importance in terms of the future prospects for families in Watts. The families of some of my students had been living in poverty for generations, giving a new meaning to the concept of the "long-term poor."

The legacy of poor single mothers in Watts may have been one of intergenerational transfer of poverty: their children were more likely to be poor and, if female, to become female heads of households. Many of my female students complained of their mothers' restrictions on their activities, asking aloud of what their mothers could be afraid. When I mentioned a few possible fears, including adolescent pregnancy and the possibility of their daughters living in poverty, they exploded, "Who is she to talk? She did! She got pregnant when she was younger than I am!" The actions of the mothers at their daughters' age seemed to reach out from the past to subtly affect their daughters' thoughts and behaviors. The daughters, once pregnant, swore they would keep their child from having a child in junior high or high school. When I spoke with these mothers and their pregnant daughters, I had the sense of two mirrors facing one another and reflecting the same image back and forth countless times. "It won't happen to my child" echoed through the generations as the legacy of adolescent maternity and its frequent companion, poverty, were passed on and on.

Adolescents cannot make rational decisions bearing upon their sexual activities in the absence of clear, detailed information on human sexuality and reproduction. The students at Medgar High more often than not possessed distorted or incorrect information. Since peer education is thought to be a particularly useful method of conveying such information to adolescents, I included a comprehensive unit on human sexuality within the peer counseling courses I taught so that my students, who were going to be speaking with their peers about issues of common concern, had correct information on pregnancy, human anatomy, and birth control. Every semester as I introduced the unit, I was amazed at how little students actually knew about sexuality and reproduction.

Among the many myths about pregnancy that were shattered each semester were such ideas as women not being able to become pregnant "the first time you do it," "if you do it standing up," "if you douche afterwards," "if you take a really hot bath," "if you jump up and down," "if you don't want to get pregnant," and "if the guy pulls out." Some of my students believed that if males did not have sex it would cause physical damage to them, so it became the obligation of the young women to have sex with them or to allow them to find another person with whom to have sex. Very few (less than 5 percent) had any idea how a woman becomes pregnant beyond a very rudimentary notion of what sexual intercourse involved, and even they exhibited a lack of knowledge and understanding of anatomy, male and female sexual functioning, and methods of protection from pregnancy and STDs (sexually transmitted diseases).

Without the knowledge of how their bodies function and how pregnancy occurs, and with a preponderance of myths surrounding pregnancy, it was not surprising that so many young women in Watts became pregnant. Those few students who did possess accurate information often engaged in pregnancy risk-taking behaviors. Apparently knowledge alone is not enough for adolescents to alter their behavior. For example, in one study of late adolescents' knowledge of AIDS, only 34 percent reported that they had changed their sexual behavior in response to the known health risk.[6] It is this phenomenon of a lack of behavior alteration in the presence of knowledge that baffles those who are attempting to help young people protect themselves against sexually transmitted diseases and to delay childbearing until they are older, are with a stable partner, and are able to support a child. Certainly, it was difficult to listen to young people who possessed the facts about protecting themselves admit quite frankly to having sex without protection. They too seemed baffled by the gap between their knowledge and their actions.

Students at Medgar High did need to have access to clear information in order to give them a fighting chance at protecting themselves against pregnancy and STDs. Some of the students' parents vehemently opposed any discussion with their children of human sexuality, reproduction, and methods of protection from STDs and pregnancy. The parents felt that if no one spoke to their children about such issues, they would not find out about them and consequently would not be involved in sexual activity. The problems with such a position were apparent over and over again as I learned that daughters from the most repressive families had become sexually active. One young girl whom I met when she was in the ninth grade had difficulty convincing her parents that she should be allowed to participate in peer counseling. I met with the parents to discuss their daughter's participation and found that they were deeply religious and did not want the girl to hear or speak about sex. Over the years that I knew her, she went from being very demure and quiet to being flirtatious with peers and male teachers to being promiscuous and finally becoming pregnant. In the absence of knowledge about what causes pregnancy and what one could do to prevent it, the students at Medgar High often found that their sexual activities resulted in pregnancy. Yet it was extremely difficult to convince these parents of the dangers inherent in their children's lack of knowledge of sexual functioning.

Indeed, a group of parents picketed in front of the school, encouraging students to skip school in protest of the school's health clinic, which they condemned as an "abortion mill." The clinic, a tremendous boon for the students who often had to forgo medical attention because they could not afford it, offered services as diverse as psychological counseling, physicals, and birth control information. The fact that it did not offer abortions was ignored by the group of parents, who continued their vehement protest against it. I was surprised to see one of my students involved in the picketing in front of the school. She worked as a peer counselor at the health clinic talking with other students about issues of birth control and STDs. When her peers questioned her about what they perceived as her hypocrisy in simultaneously working at the clinic and protesting its existence, she told them her mother did not know she was working at the clinic and that she had to participate in the demonstration with her mother or risk having her become suspicious. This kind of communication between parent and child was fairly typical, with students thinking that what their parents did not know would not hurt them and parents thinking that what their children did not know would keep them safe.

An incongruity surfaced in the logic of some of the young Latino students, both male and female, whom I counseled in Watts. They were seeking counseling in regard to their sexual activities, some in fear of pregnancy, some in fear of AIDS, and when asked if they were using any protection, they explained that, according to the Catholic church, the use of contraceptives is a sin. When it was pointed out that, according to the Catholic church, premarital sex is considered a sin so that it becomes a bit of a moot point, they were truly nonplused. This kind of faulty logic was characteristic of the thinking of many Medgar High students and contributed to the disturbing condition of the school having one of the highest gonorrhea rates in the city.[7]

Most cases of adolescent pregnancy are unplanned, and it is difficult to teach young people, especially the very young, to take responsibility for using protective measures when engaging in sexual intercourse. Being prepared for sexual activity was to these students tantamount to an admission that such activity was expected, so many Medgar High students said that they were uncomfortable carrying condoms or using birth control pills, for example. Discussions about being prepared for sexual intercourse created some discomfort for my students, who worried that any prospective partner would think "that's all I was interested in all along" or that "I've slept around a lot." Furthermore, decision-making capabilities are thought to be tied to individuals' levels of cognitive development. Thus, for very young adolescents, prospective planning behaviors which would ensure the use of some form of birth control may not yet have been a part of their cognitive repertoire. Many of my students at Medgar High knew little about the reproductive process or cause-and-effect relationships. Older adolescents were more likely to use contraceptives; however, for those who only used them occasionally, the risk for pregnancy and the transfer of STDs remained distressingly high. I spoke with young women who swore they could not be pregnant because they were "on the pill." Yet when I asked them if they had ever forgotten to take their pills, they grinned sheepishly and said, "Well, once or twice, I might have forgotten." They knew what they needed to do to protect themselves against pregnancy but did not follow through so that the protection would be effective.

Pregnancy and childbearing were often considered rites of passage in Watts, much like the use of alcohol and other drugs or participation in gang activities. Many of the mothers of my students had given birth to their first child during adolescence, so early maternity seemed to be a natural course of events for their daughters, an event which heralded adulthood and adult functions. One student's mother, with whom I was close, was my age and had just become a grandmother; we were both thirty-four at the time. Many of these mothers did not understand the correlation between early maternity and continued poverty. One mother's response to her sixteen-year-old daughter's news that she was pregnant was simply "Well, I had you when I was your age. I guess you have to start sometime. You'll find a way to manage; I did." This mother had experienced tremendous difficulty over the years in providing shelter for her three children and lived, at one point, in a church, bedding her children down for the night on the pews when she had nowhere else to go. Another mother told her daughter, "At least you'll graduate from high school before the child is born. That's more than I did." Sometimes the mothers' fervent early hopes and dreams for their daughters' lives to be qualitatively better than their own simply broke down under the weight of real-life possibilities for their girls. The mothers had to accept a little improvement over their lives rather than no improvement at all, even if it fell far short of their original vision.

Young men in the inner city often view the impregnation of a girlfriend as an achievement, a way of feeling like a man,[8] and Watts was no exception in this. Adolescents at Medgar High too often thought they could attain manhood or womanhood through sexual activity, impregnation, and childbearing. One of my students proudly showed me his infant son, saying, "You didn't think I had a kid, did you?" The implication to this statement was that he had accomplished something by fathering a child. Then, just as proudly, he said he had another child on the way by a different young woman. He was unemployed, did not finish high school, and lived with his aunts. He was not involved with his child as a primary caregiver, did not contribute to the support of the child, and only occasionally took care of him. Thus, his pride was in the fact that he had fathered two children, not in his social role as father to the children. Becoming a father, then, took on a largely biological role and served as a marker to his manhood. The tragedy was that young men in Watts often had few ways of asserting their manhood.

The lack of positive male role models in Watts was a serious problem, one which was so widespread and well acknowledged when I taught at Medgar High that the local schools had programs in which African American and Latino men spoke at assemblies of male junior high and senior high school students. Speakers talked about the meaning of "being a man" and tried to dispel the pervasive inner-city myth that begetting a child is proof of manhood. However, such a broad-brush approach did not offer the kind of individualized same-sex attention to young males that was so lacking in Watts. An assembly is very different from a long-term intimate relationship with an older, same-sex role model, a stable father who remains after the child's birth to fulfill the social role of father. The young man I knew who was most articulate on these issues and clearest in his rejection of paternity as defining manhood came from a home in which he lived with his father and sister. His father was a strong, stable, positive role model. This student was fortunate; he had what many young men in Watts did not have: a father who was an active parent.

Young boys in Watts often went from female-headed households to female-headed classrooms at the elementary schools, incorporating the same messages from their opposite-sex caregivers. It does not take a large intuitive leap to see that young males raised in Watts in female-headed households had few male role models on which to pattern themselves as fathers; if their fathers were not present, then it seemed logical that they as fathers should occupy the same roles, that of passive, and often absent, parents.

Programs like one in Washington, D.C., which pairs African American professional men with children at a poor inner-city elementary school,[9] can help to provide some of the mentoring and alternative, positive role models so lacking in young boys' lives, but once again, the assignment of mentors to young inner-city boys does not deal with the underlying problem of why they should need a mentor in the first place and does not establish the intimate relationship children have with their primary caregivers. It also does not provide the day-to-day model for positive parenting provided by a live-in parent, step-parent, or guardian.

Lacking such a positive parenting model, many young men in Watts either decided not to be involved with their children or found they were unable to assist in any meaningful way because of their high rate of unemployment. Further, their route toward paternal involvement was effectively nullified when the adolescent mother returned to her family upon the birth of a child, as many young mothers I knew in Watts did, making it difficult for young fathers to take on an active parenting role. In one case, a teenage girl at Medgar High became pregnant and married the baby's father before the child was born. However, she continued to live with her parents throughout the pregnancy, seeing her husband only occasionally. She delivered the child without his presence or support but rather with that of her mother. Ultimately, she divorced him for his lack of involvement in her life. As she spoke to me about the situation, it became clear that she did not see that he had little access to becoming involved in her life when she chose not to live with him after marriage.

Even if she had chosen to live with the child's father, their life together would not necessarily have been smooth. The high unemployment rate and the young people's lack of skills often left young couples I knew in Watts with no option but to live with one of their families. If the young woman's family was nonsupportive or unstable, and the couple lived with the young man's family, the transition could be a healthy one. In this way, adolescent pregnancy can result in the formation of a more stable family for these young mothers.[10] However, the opposite also occurred: some young women felt like outsiders, were uncomfortable with their boyfriend's mother or other family members, or were criticized for their caretaking of the new baby. Sometimes family members viewed the young woman and the new baby with outright hostility because of the added burden they placed on the strained family resources. One young woman I knew stayed almost entirely in her boyfriend's room when she was at "home" because of the animosity the family, in particular the mother, felt and demonstrated toward her. She stayed at school as late as she could each day to avoid going home.

Because the young people at Medgar High frequently did not form long-term relationships with their partners before engaging in sexual intercourse, it was not uncommon for them to separate or "break up" once a diagnosis of pregnancy was confirmed. The choices of the pregnant young women included single or joint active parenting, adoption, abortion, or shared parenting in which a relative assisted, often in a major way, with the upbringing of the child, as will be explained later in this chapter in the discussion of generational blurring.

Young prospective fathers in Watts sometimes objected to abortion, wanting a child to be born as a tangible demonstration of their manhood. If the mother decided to keep the child, the father could function as an active or passive parent; that is, he could be a primary caregiver of the child, or he could occasionally see the child and not participate in its care. Several young mothers I knew in Watts defined (with great sincerity) a good father as one who "brings Pampers [disposable diapers] and baby food once a week." All too often in Watts, adolescent fathers adopted such passive parenting roles, sometimes at the behest of the women, sometimes as a matter of their own choice, circumstances, or socialization. Young women in Watts who bore children out of wedlock often did not seek support from the children's father, and the family was then reliant upon whatever income these women could generate. When the woman was young, had not finished high school, and lacked the skills or training necessary to secure employment, that income was paltry at best, often resulting from minimum wage jobs or government aid. It was rare in Watts to find an adolescent father who paid child support. Most frequently, the burden of support fell on the young mother and her family. It is also important to note that some young women I knew in Watts wanted to become pregnant, and, once pregnant, they wanted nothing further from the child's father. As one of my students said when I asked about her baby's father, "Him? I don't want anything from him. I've got *my* baby."

Abortion and adoption were not often considered viable options among my students in Watts. They frequently said that abortion was "what white girls did" when they became pregnant, meaning that it was not what African Americans and Latinas did. Indeed, they were less likely to terminate a pregnancy than white adolescents. This is not to say that students at Medgar High never chose abortion in response to the confirmation of a pregnancy. I knew several young women who decided to have abortions. One made her decision when she realized her boyfriend would not stand by her in terms of financial support and continuation of their relationship, although he wanted her to have the baby. Another was college bound and had an abortion in order to be able to attend the prestigious university to which she had been accepted.

In general, the young women I knew in Watts had little motivation to consider abortion or adoption as a result of the lack of social stigma attached to out-of-wedlock, adolescent pregnancy within the community and, in some cases, the strong disapproval and condemnation of abortion. Children having children retains a social stigma within many white ethnic communities in this country, whereas in Watts and other inner-city communities, it is more widely tolerated. Young women see their friends with babies, and young women's families often are not disapproving of their pregnancies,[11] so little social impetus exists to refrain from early childbearing. However, even with this widespread attitude of tolerance toward adolescent pregnancy, some young women came to me when they found out they were pregnant and were worried about how they would tell their parents or guardians. In a few cases, they were disowned by their families for being pregnant, literally turned out of the house. In most others, however, the pregnancy was accepted, sometimes with resignation, sometimes with joy. Adolescent pregnancy was a common occurrence in Watts, and babies and children were, for the most part, highly valued, so the advent of an additional child was generally not viewed as a catastrophe.

In the past in much of the Latino community in Watts, an out-of-wedlock pregnancy was often a source of family disgrace and the cause of an immediate marriage. Within the African American population, adolescent out-of-wedlock pregnancy was more socially acceptable. A kind of passive sharing of certain values and mores occurred across the African American and Latino populations in the Watts community, with the result being a community-wide acceptance or at least tolerance of adolescent out-of-wedlock childbearing. Some young Latinas at Medgar High who, because of their religious or family training, had no intention of having premarital sex and who vehemently denied wanting to have children until they were older and married, gradually accepted the idea of premarital sexual activity, became pregnant, and had a child.

Ethnically encapsulated environments such as that found in Watts may also contribute to a greater tolerance of unmarried mothers. Attitudes about adolescent out-of-wedlock births may be linked to social and economic status within a community; individuals within low-income families, like many in Watts, who perceive few possibilities may have less reason to refrain from early childbearing because they perceive they have little to lose.[12] Female adolescents who possess goals for the future and are involved in school are more likely to use contraception and to choose abortion if they become pregnant.[13] In Watts, where there was a dearth of viable future opportunities, young women often perceived that they had little reason to refrain from early maternity. Adolescent pregnancy could not interfere with their plans for a bright future when no such future was envisioned.

Although widespread community acceptance or tolerance of early childbearing existed in Watts, adolescent maternity hampered individuals' chances for educational, social, and ultimately economic advances. Adolescent maternity is commonly associated with an increased risk of noncompletion of schooling, larger family size, and a disproportionate reliance on public assistance, all of which contribute to young mothers' decreased chances for economic viability. Early pregnancy is cyclical, as are so many of the problems associated with life in inner-city communities like Watts. Thus, a woman who began to have children during her teenage years was more likely to see the pattern repeating itself as her children achieved childbearing capability. Further, female-headed households make up almost half of the poor in this country, with most of the nation's poor residing within them, including almost 75 percent of all poor African American children.[14] Children in Watts living in households which were supported by these single women were all too often, by definition, children living in poverty.

The young women at Medgar High in Watts who were at risk for pregnancy were frequently easy to spot. Teachers at the school could identify behaviors which they viewed as precursors to pregnancy. Young girls became increasingly provocative in their behavior with boys, often acting out in very childish ways that reminded me of the attention-getting actions between girls and boys I saw on the playground at the elementary school across the street. Other girls, watching them, would shake their heads and say, "Ummm. She's asking for it," or "She's going to turn up pregnant soon."

Often, these behaviors were observed in girls who were not particularly successful in school. For students who had never achieved, who had not been able to succeed in school, who were in fact failing or falling behind their peers, the production of a child was considered an achievement of which they could be proud. They became the center of attention as their peers admired the baby, their accomplishment. The babies were handed around and admired at the school. For some, it was a chance to receive some desperately needed attention. One young woman was excited to have a baby because the infant received gifts of stuffed animals with which the mother loved to play. A child herself, she enjoyed the toys her infant daughter received. For those young women who were lacking love in their lives, a child was a person of their own to love.

Another cause of purposeful pregnancy risk-taking behaviors was that these young students tended to view pregnancy as a tie that would bind together two people. Young women at Medgar High in Watts at times consented to unprotected intercourse under the assumption that their boyfriends would then stay with them if they became pregnant, that indeed having a child would make their relationship permanent. All too often, however, the reverse was true. Students who became pregnant under this fallacious assumption could be observed sitting at the lunch tables at school, looking very pregnant and very miserable as they watched their ex-boyfriends interacting with their new girlfriends. Some cases of jealous retaliation occurred in which the new girlfriend punched the pregnant ex-girlfriend in the stomach, at times causing a miscarriage or a premature delivery. Such a display was vicious and at first seemed incomprehensible. However, when children of fourteen or fifteen were involved in sexual relationships which resulted in pregnancy, the fact remained that they were children and were apt to respond in childish ways.

Every year at Medgar High, prior to graduation, young women who were scheduled to graduate became pregnant and either dropped out of school or were pregnant as they accepted their diplomas. Fear revolving around their sense of inadequacy in terms of possible college performance and their lack of plans for the future caused them to engage in high-risk sexual activities. Some of the students that teachers viewed with pride as being on the road to college and a new life became pregnant the last semester before graduation. "How could she? She's so bright! She knew better," teachers lamented.

Success, however, carries a price, and in Watts, the price often involved leaving the community where these students were stars to go to a university community where, the students realized, they would be competing against people who had a better education and more opportunities. They knew they would be living away from the sense of shared reality they had in Watts, and this sense of shared reality was an important component in their self-identity. For these reasons, pregnancy seemed to some to be a viable way to stop the process, to retreat, to hide. In the absence of knowledge of what life held for them after high school, being a mother was a definite and familiar social role that carried with it increased esteem in the eyes of their peers.

Over the past decade, some researchers in the social welfare field have questioned whether adolescents living in poverty, like those I knew at Medgar High, become pregnant so as to enter the social welfare system; that is, they have questioned whether girls in poverty become pregnant with the motive of receiving Aid to Families with Dependent Children (AFDC), thus increasing the number of women and their children receiving government assistance. Such a theory fuels the notion that welfare payments contribute to the rise in female-headed households. Although the current research does not bear out this supposition, policy has been dictated by it, causing the real value of welfare payments to decrease as female-headed households have increased.[15]

The reasoning behind such a supposition is pernicious and has racist and classist overtones. The idea is that women of color who live in poverty will do whatever is necessary, that is, have a baby, in order to qualify for AFDC payments, and the underlying assumption is that minority women in poverty are lazy and would rather have babies and live on welfare than earn a living wage and support their families. Those people who maintain that young women in Watts have babies for the welfare checks they receive do not understand the appalling realities of the poverty experienced by families living on AFDC. These families speak eloquently about how very difficult it is to feed, clothe, and shelter themselves on the meager amounts allotted to them.

Applying for AFDC was a response to these young mothers' new life situation, not the reason for it. It was a response they knew well because they had encountered it frequently in the lives of other women they knew who had found themselves in similar circumstances. Without skills, without an adequate education, and without jobs, their options were limited. The younger women were when they had a child, the more likely they were to be living at home as a dependent, to be still in school, and to be unskilled. Such a dependent, unskilled status immediately placed these young women at risk for living in poverty.[16] Young women at Medgar High clearly fit this description.

It is true that single mothers in Watts often sought relief through AFDC and thus began a cycle which was difficult to break, especially if they had several children. Any employment reduced their aid amount and threatened in-kind benefits. The Omnibus Budget Reconciliation Act (OBRA) passed by Congress in 1981 caused women to be dropped from the AFDC rolls, which in turn caused them to lose their entitlement to food stamps and health insurance coverage.[17] Thus, the single mothers I knew in Watts found themselves in an economic bind. Their income was low if they were working; women continue to make around sixty cents to the dollar of men's earnings, and the low minimum wage keeps unskilled women workers below the poverty level.[18] Their monthly monetary benefits were low if they were receiving AFDC as their only means of support; welfare payments have steadily declined due to inflation and actual cuts to social welfare programs in the 1980s. Finally, their income was low if they attempted to work while on AFDC, since working reduced their aid amount and possibly made their families ineligible for such in-kind benefits as Medicaid and food stamps. The painful choice between work and medical care or food stamps effectively forced women to choose to remain on AFDC, perpetuating the cycle of poverty and dependency.

For adolescent mothers in Watts, the job opportunities were often nonexistent because their early maternity interrupted their education, resulting in severely inadequate or nonexistent job skills. These young women, without the options education can provide, often saw AFDC as their only relief. Once they began to rely on AFDC for support, with a child or children to care for and in the absence of job training programs, their chances of achieving economic autonomy were slim. Young mothers at Medgar High, who had once dreamed of careers, college, and lives filled with possibilities, visibly aged as they assimilated the realization of the reality of their future. By their early twenties, they had lost the shimmer of hope that is characteristic of youth.

Adolescent maternity was not without other risks beyond the high probability of the family living in poverty. Very young mothers were less likely to realize that they were pregnant. I repeatedly heard stories in Watts about girls at the school who were pregnant but did not know it until the fourth, fifth, or sixth month of their pregnancy. Others were able to hide the entire pregnancy from their families, an action they took out of fear of their families' response or an attempt at denial of their own condition. Obviously, such situations were not conducive to quality prenatal care. The health risks to these very young mothers and their children were clear and well known. Compared to older mothers, they had higher rates of maternal mortality, miscarriage, prolonged labor, still births, premature births, and low-birthweight babies. In Watts, girls at Medgar High routinely talked about premature deliveries, difficult labor, and birth defects. I knew many young mothers whose babies needed repeated surgery and prolonged hospital care.

Pregnant adolescents are less likely to seek prenatal care and less likely to follow a healthy prenatal regimen than older, more stable prospective mothers. My students who found that they were pregnant often tried to ignore it, perhaps in the childlike hope that it would go away. Consequently, it was rare for them to seek medical attention or begin to care for themselves until they were well into the pregnancy, if at all. Behaviors that seem automatic to some, like that of seeing an obstetrician as soon as a woman suspects pregnancy, were viewed as middle-class luxuries by many of the young women I knew in Watts. Thus, Medgar

High students I knew who became pregnant often did not seek prenatal care during their pregnancy and were likely to live in poverty once their child was born because of their lack of skills, education, and job training or the lack of employment opportunities in the inner city.

The poor eating habits of adolescents I knew in Watts generally did not improve during pregnancy, a time when good nutrition is essential to the well being of both mother and developing infant. From the moment students informed me of their pregnancies, I continually counseled them about appropriate nutrition and the need for prenatal care. One young mother-to-be told me as she drank a soda and ate a large bag of potato chips for lunch, "If it's good enough for me, it's good enough for him [the baby]."

When substance abuse was added to the maternal behaviors during pregnancy, the developing infant was at risk from the time of conception. Adolescent pregnancy was at times tied to the issue of the use of alcohol and other drugs. In one study on the use of alcohol and adolescent pregnancy risk-taking behaviors, 30 percent of the respondents reported that they had used alcohol prior to having intercourse which resulted in pregnancy.[19] Certainly, use of alcohol and other drugs impaired individuals' judgment in terms of taking risks.

An additional result of adolescent pregnancy was high infant mortality. The infant mortality rate for the United States is appalling for a modern industrialized nation, placing the nation nineteenth internationally. An African American child born in the United States has less of a chance of surviving its first year than a child born in Costa Rica or Bulgaria.[20] It was not uncommon for girls at Medgar High to give birth to a stillborn infant or to lose the child within the first few months of its birth.

So how can we effectively address the problems of these young mothers at Medgar High and other inner-city schools? Clear and early sex education, family-planning assistance, and access to birth control methods would help to reduce the likelihood of first unplanned pregnancies and the rate of subsequent pregnancies, thus reducing the likelihood of long-term dependency. The need for early intervention is poignantly evident: young girls under fifteen in the United States are more likely to have a child than their agemates in any other developed country,[21] and African American adolescents are more likely to be sexually active at an earlier age and less likely to use contraceptives than white or Latina adolescents. Such behaviors place these young women at greater risk for pregnancy and poverty.

Further needs include early educational intervention, peer education, readily available birth control to help prevent unplanned pregnancies and protection to help prevent the spread of STDs, substance abuse counseling and treatment, and health care for the prospective mothers and their children.

These young women need education, vocational skills, and employment. They need to make a living wage in employment which will provide comprehensive health benefits for their families. I knew so many who despaired of ever being able to find a job; the desire to work and to achieve independence was strong, but available jobs and job training programs were rare. Some of the women I knew, the mothers of my students, worked long hours in sweatshops in the Los Angeles garment district for very little pay in order to support their families.

Accessible, low-cost child care would help to reduce the conflicts between parenting and working. Women I knew in Watts often worked part-time because of inadequate child care possibilities. Obviously, mothers who were able to work full-time earned more for their families' support.

Training for high-quality, skilled jobs was virtually nonexistent in Watts and the surrounding communities. Employment opportunities need to flourish in Watts and other inner-city communities so that heads of households have options other than dependency on AFDC, and the child care needs of these women need to be addressed in quality, low-cost, readily available public centers. Women in poverty such as the women I knew in Watts should not be forced to choose between jobs and child care, their children's fathers living at home and welfare, or working and medical care.

Child support payments from absent fathers could also help significantly to reduce the poverty level for these families, while creating government savings of from 2 to 4 billion dollars on a national level.[22] More employment would create an income for young men with which they could either actively support their families or pay child support. The loss in the Watts community of the majority of "blue-collar" jobs because of the closing of factories, which were the major employers in the community, has created a bleak unemployment picture. Unemployment among African American adults generally runs at around 21 percent, three times that of the national rate; racism may be the root of the lack of effort to ameliorate unemployment among the African American community, and there is a perception that if such unemployment existed within the white community, a massive effort to eradicate it would occur.[23] Thus, unemployment in the community has not only caused poverty and misery, but has also engendered bitterness.

Young women at Medgar High who had children often found that their options were without promise. Many continued living at home and found they were not able to finish school. Ultimately, it was the rare young woman in Watts who was able to have a child as an adolescent, finish school, and find a decent job, although many stated that this was their intention. I met these young women as they walked on the street, holding the small hands of their children, discouraged and frustrated about their inability to find a job or change their lives. Renee, a former student of mine who was twenty and who had one small son and another child on the way, shook her head and said, "I used to have me some big dreams." She sighed and continued, "But that's all over now." Renee, and others like Renee, had entered into the ranks of a set of sad statistics in this country: yet another woman as a single head-of-household who lived with her children in poverty.

FAMILY ROLES AND GENERATIONAL BLURRING

Within many families I knew in Watts, it was the children who suffered the most. Children are the least powerful members of our society, and children born into poverty are the most victimized of all; as Michael Parenti points out, "To be conceived in poverty is to suffer risks while still inside the womb."[24] Economically distressed women in Watts were less likely than economically advantaged mothers to receive prenatal care, and their children were less likely to receive adequate medical attention and immunizations. Their children were more likely to die of such causes as poor nutrition, low birthweight, and sudden infant death. Indeed, African American children are twice as likely to die before their first birthday as white children. Their mothers are three times as likely to die during childbirth as white mothers.[25]

Divorce has had an impact on families in Watts. Married women who have children are generally appointed as the custodial parent in cases of divorce. Upon the dissolution of a marriage, the family income is reduced by two-thirds, which constitutes the father's share.[26] Thus, once a marriage is dissolved, the woman finds herself with one-third of her previous household income to support herself and her children. Arbitrary child support awards coupled with nonpayment of child support by the noncustodial parent only serves to deepen the financial distress of these female-headed families.

A nuclear family may have two wage earners, one or both of whom also function as caregivers of the children. However, after a separation or divorce, the responsibility to be financial supporter and caregiver often falls entirely to one parent. Watts, like other inner cities, is becoming a matrifocal segment of society. The women I knew in Watts were often responsible for raising and providing for children, since they tended to be the stable adult member of the family unit. If child support was not paid by the noncustodial parent, the stress for the family increased as the custodial parent (who is the mother 90 percent of the time) attempted to juggle work and child care. Often the burden became too overwhelming, particularly if she was unskilled and unable to find steady work.

Single mothers in Watts had even less protection than divorced mothers. They had to establish their children's paternity in order to enter the social welfare system and to be able to receive child support, Social Security, and veterans' benefits. Children of single mothers suffer the highest rates of poverty of any group.[27] Single mothers, like divorced custodial parents, were confronted with the day-to-day issues of child raising, one of the most pressing of which was child care.

Although female heads of households are not a homogeneous group, they are all confronted with the issue of child care. Indeed, for the families I knew in Watts, the lack of readily available and affordable child care created a conflict between the need to work to ensure the economic self-sufficiency of the family unit and the need to nurture and raise the children, and these two goals were at times mutually exclusive. Thus, the dilemma between working and child care continued, a dilemma which often was resolved in Watts by the use of multigenerational caregivers.

Low-income families in Watts often functioned cooperatively, extending the definition of "family" to members beyond the primary group and to friends, creating a broadened resource base.

They were more likely to call on members of this resource base as providers of child care. Families in Watts frequently experienced what I have come to call "generational blurring"; that is, because of multigenerational child care situations, "traditional" family roles were not adhered to and blurred across generations in new and complex ways. Mothers who were working outside the home were not always able to actively parent their children and had to defer responsibility to other family members, such as the eldest child. Very young daughters gave birth and left parenting and raising of the children to their mothers and grandmothers. Watts was filled with children raised by siblings and grandparents.

The stoicism of these individuals is apparent only upon close observation of the teenager saddled with raising her siblings while trying to go to high school or the grandparent who has raised her own children and now takes on a grandchild or several grandchildren, starting the parenting process all over again, frequently while trying to work outside the home. Adolescent mothers in Watts, tremendously at risk for living in poverty, often returned to their family unit upon the birth of their children, an action which could place the subfamily at greater risk for poverty even as it provided some stability and child care assistance for the young mothers.

In Watts, some women who worked, who were single heads of households, and who did not have adequate child care possibilities turned over responsibility for the family, in particular for the care of small children, to the eldest daughter. That daughter frequently assumed complete responsibility for all chores normally associated with an active parent: the tasks of cleaning, cooking, shopping, doing laundry, and parenting siblings. In many cases, this was a necessity; there was no one else to care for the children and maintain a stable family life. In some cases, the reasons were culturally based. In either case, this responsibility could be harmful to the young person's academic career and mental health and often signaled a premature ending to an all-too-brief childhood.

The cultural aspect of generational blurring was clear with one student, Anita, a nineteen-year-old Latina who was a senior at the high school. Her mother left home after separating from Anita's father and moved into an apartment with friends. Anita's parents were both from Mexico and had created a very traditional household according to the standards of their country of birth. Being traditional meant that Anita, as the only female remaining in the home, was responsible for all housework, meals, laundry, and nurturing of her little brother. Her father and her two elder brothers did not help her with the domestic chores. In her words, her little brother was "very slow" and was unable to care for himself, much less to assist her.

When I questioned Anita one day in concern over her constant absences, she began to cry and explained the situation. Her father felt that housework was women's work and that a woman's place was to serve men; thus, as the only woman in the household, all such tasks fell to her. This left very little time for school.

Anita took care of her younger brother, bathing him, dressing him, and taking him to school daily. She cleaned house every day. Her home was spotless, and she was proud of this. She clung to the standards of cleanliness with which she grew up, standards brought from the country of her parents, fearing a loss of face if her home was a little dusty, the laundry was piled up, or dirty dishes sat in the sink. She feared this would say she was a bad woman, unable to take care of her home, and she would feel ashamed.

To attempt to help Anita let go of some of the rigid standards which kept her tied to the house and away from school was to fight cultural mores which were deeply ingrained. For some people, it would have been easy to let the family's laundry pile up, realizing that when they became tired of not having any clean clothes, they would wash them for themselves. Such a seemingly simple solution of letting the other family members fend for themselves was an impossibility to her; she could not allow dirty laundry to accumulate because this would be a marker of her inability to care for her family.

This first generation of young people who were either born in this country or who arrived as small children often experienced difficulties unimaginable to most people. Their parents retained the culture of their country of birth and remained relatively unassimilated into the dominant culture in the United States. Their children, in effect, lived in the culture of their parents' country at home and in the culture of the United States at school and at play. Some carried their biculturalism with ease. For others, however, the schism caused trauma and turmoil.

Anita was caught in this bind, a bind from which she felt she could not extricate herself. During the day, she experienced a measure of respect and equity at school. At night, she was treated as a servant, and the contrast between the two worlds caused her to feel angry, confused, and hopeless. She spoke frequently of her life as being a cage, and she did not see any way of removing herself from it. However, she refused to abandon her perceived responsibility as primary caregiver of her younger brother and her family.

Families with two parents present in the home were not immune from this need to utilize all of the family's human resources in terms of shared responsibilities for caregiving and household maintenance. One student, Mari, had parents who worked in a factory. They were away from home from early morning until late evening each day. Mari and her older sister ironed, cooked, and cleaned for the family. They took one younger brother to school and their little sister to a sitter prior to going to school themselves. When school was out for the day, they picked up their brother and sister and went home to clean, cook dinner, hear lessons, help with homework, and teach their little sister to talk. Mari spent so much time with her little sister that she stated she felt the child was hers. Mari was, in effect, raising her.

This family was unique in the strong emphasis the parents placed on their children's education, and it was through the combined efforts of all family members that the family survived. The parents continued to work long hours to enable their children to concentrate on home and school. They did not want their children to work while in school. They sacrificed time with their children and their own health in strenuous labor in order to provide, as they said, a "better future" than they had as young people. The three eldest children have been attending college, and Mari just recently graduated with a double major.

Another aspect of generational blurring was seen in the older people who had already raised a family. Often in Watts, grandmothers took on parenting roles when their children were unable or unwilling to take care of their offspring. These grandparents greeted a very different world from the one in which they grew up or the one in which they nurtured their own children. The stressors of taking on active parenting roles for their children's children were doubly harsh, compounded by such previously unknown factors as AIDS and new and dangerous drugs. In Los Angeles, some of these grandmothers went through a training program to help prepare them for the rigors of parenting in the 1990s.

In Watts, in times of great stress, it was often members of the extended family who stepped forward to help shoulder parenting and caretaking responsibilities. The mother of one of my students experienced psychological difficulties in which she was completely unable to cope with work or her family; she had three children, one of whom was severely handicapped and was a victim of fetal alcohol syndrome. The grandmother took in all three children rather than allow them to go into foster care.

In another case, one which had a heartbreaking repetitiousness, the mother took in all of her drug-addicted daughter's children. Tasha, one of my students, was the youngest sister of the troubled, drug-addicted woman. She related to me the story of her sister, who would trade sex for drugs, who had been to jail, and who never came home except when she needed money or was pregnant. Tasha's sister had delivered five children over the years. Two of them, close to Tasha's age, had been raised with her. All the children had different fathers. The youngest child was an infant of a few months, and the grandmother was extremely concerned that her daughter was HIV positive and had transmitted the virus to the baby.

Once Tasha spoke of her mother's reasons for continuing to take in the children, saying, "Sometimes she talks about it. She just feels that she is their grandmother, they are her blood, and if she doesn't take them, then the welfare people will just split them all up and put them in foster homes. She said she couldn't live with that." The dignity of the value that blood takes care of its own even at tremendous personal sacrifice is difficult to deny. Tasha respected her mother for this attitude while ruing the fact that her sister was being allowed to create such stress in their lives. Whereas Tasha was able to graduate, leave home, and begin college, her mother's life was another story: after having raised one family, she had to raise another, including a small baby. This she did by choice; she provided a home for five children who were not hers but who were her blood relations so that they could remain together as a family.

Like the many young women in Watts who functioned as parents to their younger siblings, the older relatives who became primary caregivers to children not their own made huge sacrifices. It was common for families in Watts to take in not only grandchildren but also a niece or nephew, a friend of a son or daughter who was in need, or an entire family who had hit hard times and had nowhere to go. Children doubled up in their beds, blankets were spread on couches, and family members slept on the floor to make room for the newcomers. One family I knew took in their niece and nephew as babies when the children's mother deserted them, providing them with a loving, supportive home. Another made room for six people, my student's uncle's entire family, when they had lost their home, and they remained there until they were again financially stable. Families already living in poverty often accepted the addition of another person to their household, in spite of the obvious added burden. For those living on the borderline of financial well being, this addition was sometimes just enough to tilt the balance and cause the family to slide into poverty.

Problems existed on either side of the generational blurring equation within families who had multiple caregivers. Children raised in families which consisted of multigenerational parenting figures were often confused by the multiplicity of authority figures. In short, they were not sure who was really in charge. Caregivers in conflict over child-rearing issues created further confusion and discomfort for the children, especially for children who perceived themselves in the middle between two parenting figures, such as a grandparent and an adolescent mother or an adult mother and a caregiving older sibling.

Many of the adolescent caregivers I knew in Watts suffered great frustration when adults gave the adolescents authority and responsibility for the primary care of siblings, only to countermand that authority at their discretion. My students frequently complained that their parents required adult behaviors of them in terms of household chores and care of younger siblings but did not give them the authority they needed to deal with the children in their care. Parents who may have felt guilty about the lack of time they spent with their children sometimes compensated for it by being lenient when they were at home, and they did not back up their oldest child's disciplinary measures. The younger children then saw no reason to listen to their older siblings, since they could foresee no visible consequences for misbehavior, and this caused tremendous friction, anxiety, and conflict. Thus families with multiple caregivers were not without pitfalls, and, if dysfunctional, could create emotional and behavioral problems for the children involved. However, those which were healthy literally saved the life of the family.

Some of my students had no family in this country. They came from the trauma of war-torn countries in Central America and were sent here for their own safety, accompanied perhaps by a cousin or a sibling but often without their parents. The difficulties of becoming accustomed to a new country and learning a new language were compounded by the absence of their families. One student, Miguel, went through periodic depressions, and when I asked him about his feelings, he struggled to put them into words. "It's difficult," he would say with tears in his eyes. He deeply missed his mother and worried constantly about her safety. Miguel, like other students, benefited from the "family" created at school.

The "future teacher" and "peer counseling" programs I began and ran at Medgar High unintentionally became a sort of extended family for many of my students. This family grew and flourished, engendered by the students' needs. Thus, my students expanded my role beyond that of teacher and friend, and they adopted one another, were mentors to the younger ones, and argued like siblings. The walls of our classroom were covered with the hundreds of photographs I had taken, a family album spread out across the room.

For those students like Miguel who had no family in the community, the family at school was of particular importance. On my last day at Medgar High, Miguel did not come to tell me good-bye. I later learned that he had stood outside my door, unable to come in because he was afraid that he would break down. He had already experienced too many good-byes and could not face another.

FAMILIES IN CRISIS

Whereas many of my students' families found ways to maintain stability, some collapsed beneath the weight of intense personal crises and stress. The children carried the burdens of their families' difficulties to school, where, if they were fortunate, a teacher would devote time and attention to them, providing them with a chance to talk about their troubles.

From the beginning of my tenure at Medgar High, I heard stories of personal and family tragedy that were heartbreaking. When it was possible, I intervened, making telephone calls to a trusted colleague at the elementary school who had community contacts, calling local resource agencies, giving out referral numbers for women's shelters and crisis hotlines and substance abuse counseling clinics, and explaining to students how to help a parent apply for food stamps. One student, for example, who was doing poorly in school and seemed distracted in class, had an invalid mother who could no longer work, and she and her mother were frightened by the looming prospect of homelessness and hunger. Although some would argue that intervention in such cases is not the business of teachers, that these situations should be left to social workers and social welfare case workers, it is the classroom teachers who are in daily contact with students' needs and who thus are required to expand their roles to include those of parent, confidant, social worker, counselor, referral agent, and nurse. In short, caring teachers and administrators in Watts did what they needed to do to promote the well being of their students under the guiding principle that the role of educators is to teach, and that learning cannot occur when students' physical or emotional well being is in jeopardy. Thus, students' family crises did indeed impinge upon the classroom in a multitude of ways which required the response and attention of responsible and committed educators.

A classic example of this kind of caring occurred at the elementary school across the street from Medgar High. An interim principal collected clothing and shoes which she distributed to children who arrived at school without appropriate or necessary attire. She collected food and invited local parents who were in need to come to the school to pick up bags of groceries with which to feed their families. She explained that she responded to the needs of her students under the principle that a cold, hungry, or frightened child needs to be warmed, fed, or comforted before any attempts at instruction can begin.

This person's approach to her interim principalship was one of compassionate caring for her students and their families, one of involvement in their lives and in the lives of the people in the community. A child came to school one day saying she had only eaten beans for a week. The principal gently questioned the child and discovered that her father had left the family. Since he was the one providing for the family, they had no income after his departure. The mother was trying to feed her children with the little food she had left. The mother did not speak English, and she did not know about the public assistance programs available to her family. The principal took bags of groceries to her, contacted a community person to help her sign up for all benefits for which her family was entitled, and let her know she was not alone. This model of com-

passionate caring well beyond the classroom was evident throughout Watts, and it was just such behavior that helped to mitigate
some of the cases I observed of what initially appeared to be
neglect. These cases often stemmed from a lack of family resources
rather than the parents' lack of appropriate nurturing behaviors.

One form that family crises took was child abuse. Child abuse
is not a new social ill. Baby and child battering, infanticide, and
neglect have a long history. A literature study can turn up evidence
of the abuse of children in works from Shakespeare to fairy
tales.[28] Indeed, with reported child abuse cases in the United
States having increased from 600,000 in 1979 to 2.4 million in
1989,[29] it is obvious the problem is escalating. By the end of my
first year at Medgar High, I had confronted child abuse so often
that it seemed almost commonplace. In my journal written during
my second month at the high school I wrote the following:

> I had a student tell me yesterday that she missed school because
> she has to see her counselor on Thursdays. She told me, "I have
> to [see the counselor] because I was molested by my step-sister's
> father." She said this with no apparent bitterness in her voice. It
> was simply a fact of life for her: He did this so now I have to see
> a counselor on Thursdays. "I just wanted you to know where I
> am on Thursdays, that's all," she said. I nodded, murmured a
> few words of comfort to her, and gave her a hug. I made a note
> in my gradebook and started talking to the class about punctu-
> ation. Watts may unhinge me.

Although I had some experience in dealing with child abuse
when I taught in Oregon, I was not prepared for the frequency of
reported abuses my students brought to me. The amount of family
violence I encountered in these students' lives was tremendously
troubling, and I exerted much effort to trying to understand its
genesis. I need perhaps to reiterate that I was in a unique position
at Medgar High: because I taught classes designed around human
services and helping others, my relationship to students was one
which allowed them to confide in me and seek out my assistance,
a role I was teaching them to fulfill for their peers. Further, administrators and other teachers called on me for assistance in helping
troubled students. Consequently, my experiences were not reflective of those of the typical classroom teacher at Medgar High.

The families I knew living in poverty in Watts were under significant stress. Unemployment was rampant, causing families to

seek government assistance in the form of housing, food stamps, Medicaid, and AFDC as a means to provide food, medical care, and shelter. Research shows that those who are most at risk for abusing children include young parents, single mothers, unskilled or unemployed individuals, those who are poorly educated or socially isolated, those who live in poverty in poor housing and who are dependent on social welfare programs, and those who have poor marital relationships or who are abusing alcohol.[30] However, because the list of risk factors includes characteristics which were readily found in the Watts community, there was a danger of drawing conclusions about the potential abusiveness of the community members as a group. In such a fashion is racial prejudice perpetuated; that is, observations, whether true or false, made about a small segment of the population are generalized to describe the entire population. The vast majority of Watts residents I knew, many of whom had lives which reflected a number of the risk factors described earlier, were not abusive parents.

Child abuse cases are situationally specific. Thus, the presence of any one of these characteristics does not predispose an individual to becoming abusive. A combination of characteristics may result in life situations which can potentially lead to abusive behavior. For example, a parent may be doing an excellent job until the addition of another child who is sickly or demanding or whose delivery was very difficult for the mother. The addition of the extra stressors may create a potentially volatile situation, touched off by a triggering event.

Several points are important to consider when attempting to understand family violence in inner-city communities. Inner-city residents like those in Watts interact with government and public service agencies much more frequently than their wealthier counterparts, and thus they are under closer scrutiny. Further, statistics about child abuse reflect *reported* cases of abuse. Although there is some evidence that lower socioeconomic status, like that experienced by many families in Watts, is positively associated with abusing parents,[31] the issue may be more complex than what it appears on the surface. Whereas child abuse cases may be reported more frequently among those who live in poverty, the reporting may be a significant issue. People living in poverty in Watts were often unable to afford private medical care. They used health care facilities which were provided by the county, and, although all medical doctors are mandated reporters, the doctors at such facilities may be more likely to report cases of suspected child abuse than private practioners, whose patients derive from middle- to upper-class families. Thus, it may be easier to hide cases of child abuse in higher-income families. Finally, parent-hood can be quite stressful even under ideal circumstances. Many families living in poverty in Watts were headed by single women who had to bear an enormous burden of stress as the sole care-giver of their children. Because child abuse is situationally specific, the presence of these stressors in the form of risk factors can increase an already stressful situation to the point where violence is more likely. Thus, it was not the residents of Watts or other inner-city communities who were predisposed to abusive behavior but their communal presence in a stressful situation which increased the risk.

Some parents in Watts who were living in poverty did not see the means to better their lives and experienced hopelessness. This hopelessness caused some of them to turn to alcohol and other drugs as a source of solace or escape. People under the influence of alcohol or other drugs may be more disposed to uncontrolled behaviors, and their children may bear the brunt of their lack of self-control. However, it is important to note that no causal rela-tionship has been established between the use of alcohol and other drugs and spouse or child abuse.

One student, Aracely, talked about her alcoholic and abusive father, an unhappy man frustrated with his life situation. He attempted to escape his unhappiness through heavy alcohol con-sumption. When his children were small, they hid from him when they heard him arrive home inebriated. Aracely spoke of huddling together with her brother and little sister under a bed, the three of them holding one another and trembling until they heard him finally go to sleep. They knew they were safe then. Later, when they were adolescents, they no longer cowered when he came home after he had been drinking. Aracely said that he knew that they could retaliate in self-defense, and so he confined himself to verbal abuse.

Such abuse is clearly tied to family power issues, with the per-petrators continuing their abuse until a shift in the power balance occurs. Some of my high school students in Watts who reported battering or threats of battering stated that when their parents attempted to hit them as they had when they were small, they were able to ward off such attacks because they were "too big now."

All the cases of abuse that I reported involved young women. The young men who spoke to me of attempted abuse were saved, perhaps, by their physical size, which often kept their mothers from inflicting injury and which helped them to actively fend off an attack from their fathers.

It is important to note that teachers are "mandated reporters" of child abuse; that is, they are required by law to report all cases of suspected abuse. California Penal Code (Section 11166) requires that all certificated employees and those who are employees of child care facilities must report any incidence of suspected child abuse. Los Angeles Unified School District (LAUSD), which includes the community of Watts, went beyond the requirements of the state of California in terms of mandated reporters. LAUSD required that *all* employees of the district report such suspected abuse. Thus, teachers became involved in the most intimate details of a family's life and of closely guarded family secrets.

The reporting of child abuse was not without controversy. Some individuals felt that mandatory reporting increased the likelihood of false reports, those reports in which children falsely state that they have been abused or in which mandated reporters report in good faith a case of suspected abuse which ultimately is found to be without merit. A large measure of intercultural sensitivity is necessary in the assessment of suspected child abuse, particularly in situations in which the children involved are of color and are poor and the reporter or child care worker is white[32] and is of a different socioeconomic class. Multicultural sensitivity to differing norms for family interactions is essential.

A clear example of the need for caution and cultural sensitivity in reporting suspected abuse occurred with one student at the high school, a Latina, who had been traumatized at age ten when an anonymous party reported to the police that the girl's father was sexually molesting her. The girl's mother had abandoned the family. The girl lived with her father in a small garage which had been converted to a one-room apartment where, at night, they slept together in the same bed, the only bed they owned. Someone perceived their sleeping arrangement as being sinister and filed a report. At eighteen, she finally spoke of the event. She said the police had come at night and had taken her from her father. She was subjected to questioning about his behavior toward her and ultimately was given a physical which included a pelvic examination and tests for the presence of semen in her vagina. Although she vehemently denied that he had ever touched her in any way other than that of a competent father tending his young daughter, she was forced to undergo the examination, which horrified her and left her, at ten years old, feeling that she had been raped. Her comment was that this incident had spoiled the innocence of her relationship with her father, which was never the same again. It was eventually decided that the charges were unfounded. Whereas the legal system was able to dismiss and in essence forget the charges, this young woman was not able to do the same.

The possibility of false reports imposes an even greater need for intercultural sensitivity in reporting suspected child abuse. However, mandated reporting remains at the forefront of measures for the protection of children's well being, and I was grateful for my status as mandated reporter because it enabled me to intervene in situations in which my students were being hurt and required help, support, and protection.

Abused children do exhibit behaviors which are indicative of their plight. Such behaviors as thumb sucking or rocking, aggressiveness or extreme compliance, or discomfort with physical contact, to name just a few, may be indicators of possible abuse. Every year in Watts, I had students in my classes who sucked their thumbs. Some of their teachers made comments about these students "acting like a baby," evidently not realizing that clear reasons existed for such regressive behaviors and that they can be flags for the informed classroom teacher, indicators of deeper problems.

The causes of family violence in Watts varied and were as diverse as the families themselves. Those abusers who were male may have been influenced by a rigid adherence to the notion of a patriarchal family. Within a "traditional" family in some cultures, a dominant/submissive power relationship may exist in which the male holds the power and creates a structure of appropriate behavior.[33] He may perceive force as a realistic remedy for coping with a family member who is behaving in what he deems an inappropriate manner. The male within this patriarchal family may maintain the perspective seen throughout history of children as being part of the father's property, a common perception among traditional Latino parents in Watts. An often repeated cry from students when they reported being hurt by a parent was that the parent said, "You are my child. I gave you life, and I can take it back." The students felt powerless to protect themselves. When they found out that they were protected under the law, they expressed both fear at the possible repercussions of betraying a family secret and relief that the abuse might possibly stop. Thus, culture played a part in child abuse. What was considered abusive according to the law in this country was at times considered a parental right to discipline by parents from other countries. Several of the child abuse cases with which I dealt in Watts revolved around such cultural differences.

Cultural clashes in Watts often prefaced instances of family violence. Men from cultures in which families were patriarchal and in which the father's word was law were shocked when their children assimilated values from their peers that were at odds with the values taught in the home. They perceived their children as being disrespectful of them. As my adolescent students began to strive for more independence, as they began to reject their parents' mores, some of their fathers became more authoritarian and resorted to physical force in an attempt to control them. In particular, clashes between fathers and daughters were common. Daughters who were particularly vulnerable were those who rejected the morality and expectations of their parents' birth country and decided to date, especially if they chose someone of a different ethnicity or race or refused to conform to the culturally determined traditions of courtship accepted by their parents; those who became sexually active; or those who rejected the accepted post–high school role of wife and mother in lieu of a college education.

Factors which increase the risk of mothers mistreating their children include youth, single marital status, unwanted pregnancy, the presence of other children in the home, low level of education, social isolation, and poverty.[34] Mothers who carry an unwanted pregnancy to term are especially at risk if they are adolescent, single, unskilled, and confronting the accumulated stressors of living in poverty. They are less likely to be involved in prenatal care, which increases the likelihood of giving birth to a low-birthweight infant, causing difficulty in parent-child bonding, a further risk factor.[35] This was the profile of many of the young mothers I knew in Watts.

Unrealistic parental expectations of the child may cause stressors which can lead to a violent situation. I knew such parents in Watts who were unaware of the stages of child development and who held expectations for behaviors which the child was physically or cognitively incapable of producing. Adolescent parents who had not benefited from training in child development were particularly at risk for holding unrealistic expectations of their new babies. Some expected the child to fulfill their need for being loved and nurtured and experienced disappointment and anger when the child did not fulfill these needs. Adolescent mothers whom I knew in Watts frequently expressed that their motivation for having a baby was to have someone who would love them. Thus, the child was slated to be the fulfiller of the mother's emotional needs even before its birth. When the children were born, these young mothers realized that they had to fulfill their babies' needs rather than having their own needs met. Their disappointment sometimes resulted in abusiveness.

Beyond the pressures of poverty, joblessness, and resultant hopelessness, the age of parents can be positively associated with the probability of abuse. Older parents are deemed less likely to be abusive.[36] As mentioned earlier in this chapter, adolescent parenthood was common at Medgar High. Pregnancy was viewed as a rite of passage. Thus, some young women became sexually active at an early age, became pregnant, and often opted to continue the pregnancy. These young women, sometimes abused as children and adolescents, became single parents, and they were often unable to provide for the child, lacking as they were in education and marketable job skills. These very young parents, adolescents themselves, were ill-equipped to deal with the rigors and responsibilities of parenthood, with the demands of a child, especially when more than one child was involved. The young mothers I knew talked about how they "couldn't have fun anymore." They could not date or go out with friends as they had before their babies' birth. "You got to get real serious," one young mother sighed. Add to this situation the extra pressure of single parenthood while living in poverty, and the risk of abuse increased.

One of the responses to a case of child abuse was to remove the children from the home. In the cases I reported at Medgar High, the police came directly to the high school to question the abused students, to ascertain details of the abuse and its severity, and to obtain information on the locations of any other children in the family. If the officers decided the children were in danger, they placed them in a police car and immediately removed them from both school and home. Such moves were traumatic for the children, no matter how gentle the officers were. I found it extremely difficult because at that point my involvement in the case was over, and I did not know what was happening with the students who had been abused, if they were being returned to their parents or if they were being placed in foster care. From then on, all interactions with the family and the abused children were handled by those trained to deal with child abuse, that is, police or sheriff's officers, social workers, and child protection agency case workers. Such decisions as to whether a child should be removed from the family were fraught with difficulty. If social workers decide to remove children from their homes too early, they are accused of destroying family cohesion, especially within inner-city communities like Watts. If they are too optimistic in their assessments and wait too long before placing a child in foster care, they are accused of failing to protect the child and allowing the child to be injured. Because the fixation of blame in social work can result in great personal loss when the individual's assessment of potential risk factors is incorrect, social workers may take a defensive posture. This ensures their protection but may not always be in the best interests of the child and the family.[37] They appear to be in the unenviable position of possibly being wrong no matter what they do.

Once the abuse was reported and the authorities intervened, the children sometimes found themselves returned to their home and in danger again. I found that many of the cases of child abuse that I reported in Watts were not first-time incidents. Over and over again, as I filled out the child abuse report forms before calling the police to make a report, I came to the section on prior abuse and saw the students duck their heads and look away when I asked the question "Has this ever happened before?" The students answered quietly, awkwardly, that it had, although the previous incidents had not always been reported. "I didn't think anyone could ever help," one young woman said. She had bruises and punctures on her arms and legs, the exact impressions of the heel of a high-heeled shoe. On other occasions her mother had beaten her with a curling iron, the buckle end of a belt, and her fists. Thinking that no one could help her, this girl suffered in silence.

Abuse was not confined to children. Within one of the abusive patriarchal families I knew in Watts, a form of "hierarchical abuse" took place in which the husband abused the wife, who in turn abused the children. A key to unlocking this puzzle of family violence was the relative powerlessness felt by all members. The father felt powerless because of his inability to secure employment and provide for his family. This led to a sense of impotence and anger. The anger was taken out on the next person in the hierarchy, his spouse. He abused his wife, who in turn felt powerless, impotent, and angry. She took out her anger on the children, who were the next in line in the hierarchy, and the cycle of abuse continued.

The children, the least powerful, absorbed the anger from both parents and learned that to be at the top of the hierarchy, the place where no one batters you, you must be physically the strongest, the abuser not the abused. Such messages can be carried into adulthood, causing a new spiral of abuse. However, it is important to note that intergenerational transfer of violent behavior patterns, a commonly accepted concept manifested in the theory that abused children are more likely to become abusive parents, is not evidenced in actual life. Although previous abuse may place an individual at risk for becoming an abusive parent, no direct correlation between the two exists.[38]

My students did respond to the violence in their home lives, out of fear for their own personal safety or for the safety of their siblings or a parent. One student, Henry, grew tired of his father's constant badgering and emotional abusiveness, which had been going on since he was a small boy. At sixteen, Henry was six feet tall and possessed considerable physical strength. On one occasion when his father tried to hit him, Henry knocked him flat on the floor and then left the house. As he explained to me the next day, "I didn't want to hurt him, but he's got to stop this shit." He experienced tremendous guilt for having raised his hand against his father. Another student, Aracely, routinely put her body between her intoxicated and abusive father and her mother to deflect his violence from her mother. Aracely's aggressiveness, jeers, and threats usually caused him to stop and leave the house. She felt anxiety about leaving her mother alone, feeling she was the only protection her mother had and that her mother was safe as long as she was near her.

One of the most difficult areas for me in dealing with child abuse in Watts was to watch an adolescent in double pain: pain over the abuse by a father or stepfather and the perceived complicity of the mother. These young women often asked, "Why didn't she stop him? She knew what was happening." This notion of maternal complicity is a loaded one. The mother was thought to be at fault whether or not she was the active agent of abuse. Motherhood is an emotionally laden role in Western culture, and mothers are defined as being primary caregivers and nurturers of children. Thus, the mother is often considered at fault if she is the abuser or if she is unaware of or unable to stop the abuse by another adult.[39]

One case of sexual abuse with which I dealt had been happening for years, since the student, Colette, was a small child. She had been taken out of the family at one point because of allegations that her father was sexually abusing her, but she was returned to her parents. She did not speak out again because her life in the foster home had deeply frightened her, and at least in her own home, she said, she had her mother. However, her mother was unable to protect her, and her father continued to molest her for a number of years, bringing in other men to have sex with her, and eventually molesting her younger sister. Her sister reported the sexual abuse to her teacher at school the next day. Such a pattern of sexual abuse is not uncommon. Sexual abuse may begin with the eldest child when she is between six and nine and continue until the next daughter reaches the age when abuse began with her older sister, whereupon she is the next victim.[40]

Colette's mother timidly told me one day that she did not know about what had been happening, and that if she had known, she would have put a stop to it. She was sitting outside of the courtroom where the case was being tried, and I was there to support Colette and her family. I put an arm around the mother's shoulders. Whether she knew or not seemed a moot point. She too had been abused by her husband, was cowed and suffering, and had long ago given up trying to fight him. He was simply too powerful, too personally and physically overpowering. She exhibited many of the characteristics common to battered women in her fear of her husband, her feelings of powerlessness in his presence, her lack of financial resources without him, and her feelings of failure and guilt toward her two older daughters. Although it may be difficult for some individuals not involved in an abusive situation to comprehend, many women have been so immobilized and demoralized by abuse that they are unable to stop the abuse to their children and suffer their own abuse in silence as a means of simply staying alive.

Such abuse damaged the whole family, leaving no one exempt. Inside the courtroom, when the girls' father walked in, handcuffed and attended by a guard, the youngest daughter, who was three, ran up to the railing, calling, "Daddy! Daddy!" She did not understand the situation, and when her father was led away later, she asked the bailiff, "When is my daddy coming back?" The bailiff placed a hand on her head, looked up at me for a moment, then leaned down and said, "Not for a long time, honey."

Months later at school, I found Colette sitting on the stairs in front of my classroom, waiting for me. She was crying, and I sat down next to her on the step, put an arm around her shoulders, and asked her what was wrong. She said, "I think everyone knows. I think they can see it on my face." She pointed to her forehead, making me think of Hester Prynne in *The Scarlet Letter*.[41] In Colette's case, the letter she felt she wore for all to see was "I" for incest. The abuse had stopped when her father was put in prison, but its effects were far from over.

Society should not turn a blind eye to the plight of abused children. Unfortunately, law enforcement and child protection agencies in Los Angeles that routinely dealt with this problem were often so deluged with cases that it was extremely difficult for them to do an effective job. The lack of adequate foster homes, especially for children of color living in poverty, made removal of children from their families a last resort. In some cases with which I dealt, a warning from the police was sufficient to motivate individuals to modify and control their behavior. In others, removal of all the children from the home and therapy helped to rehabilitate the parents. However, some, like Colette's father, continued the cycle of abuse, leaving the survivors of such abuse feeling traumatized and scarred. In this cycle of abuse, all people merit sympathy and assistance. It is all too pat to simply blame the offending person—parent, step-parent, or guardian. The challenge is to try to break the cycle by dealing with the social ills which may contribute to this problem and by providing rehabilitation for those offending individuals and counseling for those who have been abused.

Other sources of abuse existed in Watts beyond those mentioned thus far. A society which is intrinsically violent contributes to family abuse. Violence is often viewed as an acceptable method of conflict resolution on the personal and the societal level in the United States. Self-protection and self-promotion are taught more than cooperation, and few people possess or use conflict management skills. It is not surprising that people resort to violence when confronted with conflicts, frustration, or stressors, even when small children are on the receiving end.

Whereas society professes great concern over deaths and injuries to children caused by battering and abuse, no such concern is expressed over the morbidity and mortality rates of children caused by societal neglect. Children are living in abject poverty in communities like Watts. They are malnourished and given inadequate medical care. Many of my students in Watts ate breakfast and lunch at school, the only meals some of them received. The subsidized meal program provided food to children who otherwise would have gone to class with empty stomachs. When school was out for the year, bands of small children from the Watts neighborhood showed up on the high school campus looking for food. One could argue that allowing children to go hungry surely constitutes abuse at the societal level.

Priority needs to be placed not only on protecting children from abuse by their caregivers but on protecting them from all forms of abuse. Otherwise, children will be born and sometimes die in enclaves of poverty within a country of enormous wealth, suffering from such preventable afflictions as malnutrition, low birthweight, or lack of proper medical care. As one researcher states, "As long as we tolerate a society in which some persons have barely enough resources to survive while others have far in excess of needs and enjoy extravagant consumption, we are *all* guilty of violence. If we condone poverty, we condone violence."[42] In Watts, abuse and violence at the societal level were dramatically clear.

When people feel powerless within society, they may attempt to find outlets in which they can be powerful and exert power over another. Children, the least powerful of all, bear the brunt of that burden, and it is often a caring and observant classroom teacher who helps these children break free of the burden of abuse.

People interested in education continue to discuss why students in inner-city communities like Watts perform academically below the level of their agemates elsewhere. To answer this question, we must look beyond school. Education does not exist in isolation. Children do not leave their hunger, the traumas of their personal lives, their dysfunctional families, their poverty, or their emotional pain on the school's doorstep as they enter. We do not teach subjects. We teach children. In Watts, we taught young people like Mari and Anita, Tasha and Miguel, and Henry and

Colette, who were deeply affected by the social environment in which they were raised. Their family lives were an essential key to understanding them and helping them learn.

CHAPTER 3

Gangs

During my first semester of teaching in Watts, one of my seniors, Hector, came to class wearing a pair of sunglasses. Once the class was involved in their writing assignment, I stopped next to Hector's desk, smiled, and motioned for him to take off the sunglasses. He looked up and whispered, "Please don't make me." I squatted down next to his desk and said, "Hector, I won't make you do anything. What's going on?" Slowly, so that only I could see, he pulled the glasses away from his face. His eyes were swollen and blackened, the skin tightly stretched, his cheeks etched with fingers of black and blue. Hector had been severely beaten by a group of young men from a local gang. This same scene repeated itself with sickening regularity over the next four years.

Gang activity in Los Angeles continues to increase, while limited state, local, and school district programs attempt to abate its spread. Approximately two hundred gangs are in existence in Los Angeles, formed on the basis of territory or turf, and these gangs are generally ethnically or racially segregated with a membership that is highly associated with poverty.[1] Almost one hundred of these are Latino gangs.[2] Children at ages nine or ten join the "baby set" of a gang, carrying drugs, acting as lookouts, and often toting their own weapons. How this disturbing and violent trend began and why it flourishes in Watts are two of the questions which will be addressed in this chapter.

To understand present-day gang activity in Watts, and in South-Central Los Angeles in general, it is helpful to understand the genesis and history of gangs in the area. They are not the invention of the 1980s, although the media coverage of gangs in Los Angeles was intensive throughout that decade and into the 1990s. Los Angeles gang history parallels the history of immigration of minorities into the area. In the early 1900s, Latinos, various ethnic groups from Asia, and African Americans came to Los Angeles at the behest of city officials and industrialists who were intent upon attempting to enlarge the work force. However, the new arrivals, who were not treated equitably in terms of their living conditions and education, became isolated into ethnic enclaves and began to lose hope that life would change for the better. Thus, the first condition was created in which gang activity can grow, that of people feeling disenfranchised from the dominant society.

Immigration from Mexico increased between 1910 and 1925, with people from communities in Mexico creating similar communities in Los Angeles. People in the new country banded together with those from their hometowns in Mexico, forming groups for support and entertainment. They brought with them a value of family and property, and the first gangs retained these values: insults to family or territory sparked retaliation. However, these first gangs were more akin to social clubs than to the often violent far-reaching illicit enterprises that exist today.

The Chicano gangs in Los Angeles expanded throughout the 1950s. In the late 1950s and early 1960s, because of their lack of legitimate employment and assimilation opportunities, gangs became involved in more illegal activity as they moved into drug sales, in particular heroin. The 1960s saw the increase of political consciousness in the community (Brown Berets and the Chicano Power movement) and ethnic pride. Federal and state funds came into the poor communities for parks, recreational activities, and increased job training programs, alternatives to life on the streets. Although violent activities decreased at this time in New York City and Washington, D.C., which were major media focal points, violence in Los Angeles continued to grow through the 1960s, 1970s, and 1980s, especially as social conditions once again deteriorated and funds for social programs were cut. Some of the young again began to feel a sense of hopelessness and despair. They confronted depressing voids in their lives, voids which have existed for them throughout this century and which bear a striking resemblance to those experienced by the young in Watts today: lack of education, lack of jobs, lack of housing, and lack of hope.

The African American gangs in South-Central Los Angeles are more recent and less well documented than their Latino counterparts. It was after World War II that membership in African American gangs began to increase. They started with the Slausons, a gang which spawned some members of the Black Panthers. The history of African American gangs is similar to that of Chicano gangs in the 1950s and 1960s. The social programs, the Black Power movement, and black pride pulled some young people off the streets, although gang violence continued to escalate in Los Angeles through the 1960s.

In the late 1960s, a gang called the Crips began to become active, at first as a small gang at Fremont High School just outside of the Watts community.[3] Crip members wore earrings, were known for their physical attacks on other African American youth, and were considered extremely violent. As their legend spread, other young people banded together and adopted the Crip color blue. They too were involved in violent activities, and an opposing gang formed for protection from them. This anti-Crip group became known as the Bloods and claimed red as their color.

New weapons came onto the scene, including sawed-off shotguns and automatic weapons, and the homicide rate started to spiral upward. Whereas older gang members (called OGs or original gangsters) had used physical strength to fight their battles, the gang members of the late 1980s and early 1990s "come from the pocket," using a knife or a gun with which to fight,[4] and the use of such weapons immediately escalated the level of violence and damage, neither of which was confined to adolescent and adult gang members. At a local junior high school down the street from Medgar High, the gang problem, including gang violence, was one of the school's primary concerns. Even at the elementary school across the street, small children "threw" gang signs (made the hand signals of a particular group), claimed membership in a "set" or a subgroup of a particular gang, became "taggers" (people who wrote gang-related graffiti on the walls and on city buses), and "showed colors" (wore the color associated with a particular gang, often in the form of a "rag" or bandana).

The feud between the Crips and the Bloods intensified in violence throughout the 1980s and into the 1990s. The gangs continued to expand into suburbia as they searched for new markets for drug sales,[5] bringing with them their well-known signature: drive-by shootings, violence, and death. Some consider the "gang-bangers" or gang members to be "expendable" or "throwaway kids," not worth the trouble it would take to reclaim them. The problems they cause are real and troubling, as are the socioeconomic problems in U.S. society which created the conditions in which gangs were able to flourish. However, the stories gang members tell of their reasons for joining a gang illustrate that it is too simplistic to view gangs as being the activity of "bad kids."

What factors in their environment would cause the young people I knew in Watts to join a gang? The question would be easier to answer if it asked what was missing from their environment that caused them to join a gang. The young people I knew in Watts spent hours every day in front of the television, drinking in messages about life in America. They saw that many people had nice homes or nice cars, enough to eat, fashionable clothes. Television presented the idea that this was the "American Dream" to which they were entitled, but a piece of this dream was denied them through "legitimate" means. They had been poorly educated. They lived in poverty. Teenage unemployment in the inner cities in this country can run as high as 70 percent,[6] and those jobs the young people were able to secure (working in fast-food restaurants, clerking, or bagging groceries) offered limited hours, minimum wage, few benefits if any, and little hope for the future. Their families were often dysfunctional. They were, as a people, suffering from decades of neglect, ethnic encapsulation, and academic poverty. Watts seemed to have an invisible yet palpable wall around it that kept in the poor and disenfranchised. Having been effectively excluded from the opportunities available in the dominant society, their response was to create their own society. If they were not able to possess the tools with which to earn a part of America's material wealth, then they found alternative methods to secure it.

One of my students who was a gang member wore brand-new and expensive running suits, and sported weighty gold nugget rings on his fingers and inch-thick ropes of gold chains around his neck. He drove a new car. He once said he thought teachers were suckers because we worked so hard for so little pay: he could make a teacher's monthly salary in a week, he maintained. The thought that a teacher was likely to live longer and had less of a chance of dying a violent death or being arrested and incarcerated did not seem to deter him. What was the point in trying to get one of the scarce legitimate jobs when it would only pay minimum wage? By selling drugs, he was able to purchase the things he wanted, his piece of the pie, and to help his family. He was a provider, a role all too often denied African American males in this society.

When I first began to teach in Watts, I taught a senior remedial English class. We were discussing paragraph development one day when I heard a beeping noise. A student stood up and began to sidle toward the door, saying, "I gotta' go. No offense. I just gotta' go now." He was very polite, attempting to make sure I knew it was not my lesson on paragraphs that caused him to leave the room. I was completely baffled and turned to my class for some explanation. They explained, amused by my obvious confusion, that the student who had left was a gang member and was selling drugs, and the noise I had heard was his pager or beeper. He had probably been paged, they told me, by either his supplier or a customer, either of which required his immediate response.

This young man, who was charming and warm in class, read and wrote at the fourth-grade level, carried a beeper, and had politely left my classroom to deal with a drug transaction. It was because of such situations that the rules at Medgar High seemed so mysterious and incomprehensible to the outsider: no beepers allowed on campus, no blue or red shoe laces, no blue or red or purple clothing, no baseball caps, no rags, no earrings, no braids. A major part of one's day as a teacher could be taken up in confiscating beepers, caps, and rags and in instructing students to undo their braids, "lose" their earrings, or unlace their shoes. A teacher trying to enforce such rules begins to feel like a member of the fashion police.

Indeed, part of my frustration in teaching at Medgar High revolved around establishing a common code of conduct upon which the Future Teachers, the Peer Counselors, and I could agree, especially for those who worked with the children at the elementary school. What seemed obvious to me in the first two years of the programs was not necessarily obvious to some of my students. One day, for example, I received an urgent phone call from my colleague and friend at the elementary school who worked as the liaison between our two schools for the programs I ran. She said, "Ann, you'd better get over here." I hurried across the street to the school to discover that one of my Future Teachers was wearing tennis shoes on which she had proclaimed her gang affiliation in ink. This had entirely escaped my detection as I took roll and walked the class to the elementary school to work with the children. However, the children immediately noticed it, and the classroom teacher was justifiably upset when her students began questioning my student on her gang activities.

This incident sparked a long debate as to whether gang members should be allowed into the two programs. My students and I wanted to keep the classes open to anyone interested in them and

to generate a specific code of expected conduct. We were successful in helping some students leave gang activity by keeping the
classes open. Some in the administration strongly felt that to be a
Peer Counselor or Future Teacher students must not be involved
in any gang activity, that this would be a contradiction in terms.
They had a valid point, but they did not take into consideration
the fact that involvement in the program sometimes functioned as
an incentive to change affiliation from gangs to one of our programs.

The students recognized that gang membership for protection
was sometimes a matter of survival. For some, gang membership
was a potent form of protection in a neighborhood where it was
often dangerous to be unaffiliated. Students who had to cross the
turf of rival gangs on their way to school were harassed by both
groups. Several of my students claimed that they belonged to a
gang but did not "gangbang" or participate in their activities; they
simply needed the protection that such affiliation provided. Thus,
my students differentiated between active involvement in a gang
and involvement for protection. "Peer counselors obviously can't
go around stealing or hurting people," they said, laughing at the
irony. "But if you're with a gang for protection, and you're not
gangbanging, that's different. Then you should be allowed into
the program."

The adolescents I knew in Watts joined gangs for reasons both
simple and complex beyond the serious need for protection. Some
were looking for a means of earning money, having been denied
access to traditional avenues; the appeal of making a few hundred
dollars a day makes such adolescents perfect targets for recruitment into a gang and participation in drug sales.[7] My students
reported they experienced a daily barrage of harassment from
gangs, everything from being verbally challenged to being threatened with weapons. Some of them capitulated and joined a gang
for protection; others managed to walk the very vulnerable and
dangerous middle line of neutrality.

When analyzing gang activity, a common question revolves
around the causes of the violent behavior of some of the gang
members. Such questions cannot be raised without posing the
same type of question to society in general: Why are United States
society and all too often its police forces, for example, so violent?
Young people involved in violent gang activities are influenced by
the society in which they are raised. Their violence often reflects

the violence that is in many instances an accepted part of societal interactions.

Many adolescents who become involved in delinquent activities come from families in which they were abused or neglected or both, although clearly not all those children who were abused become delinquent.[8] One study in particular reports a significant association between a childhood history of abuse and family violence and violent behaviors in adulthood.[9] Thus, one reason for some of the delinquent behaviors of adolescents in Watts may have been that they were abused as children. Violence can beget violence, and children who grow up viewing violence as a common aspect of their lives may carry such violent behaviors into adolescence and adulthood.

Research shows that many delinquent youths are multiply handicapped, having neurological impairment which may manifest itself in irritability, poor concentration, decreased attention span, and decreased impulse control.[10] Some students in Watts who became involved in gangs exhibited learning difficulties and were not given appropriate educational intervention. This caused these students to have negative school experiences, often leading them to decide to leave school at an early age, after which they were highly susceptible to involvement in gang activity.

Thus, the young people in Watts who were involved in violent activities may have been responding to a variety of factors, such as a central nervous system disorder that caused poor impulse control, a psychiatric disturbance of some type, or a history of violence between or at the hands of their parents or caregivers. It is important to reiterate that only a small percentage of those children who are abused grow up to become violent or abusive. However, of those individuals in society who are involved in violent, delinquent acts, a large percentage were abused. The picture then of cold-hearted gang members involved in violent acts for which no explanation exists is a simplistic generalization. Many possible causes exist beyond the most often cited socioeconomic ones.

Gang affiliation provided some tangible advantages for the young gang members I knew in Watts. Gang members had access to cash; received increased prestige, peer support, and protection; and gained increased power in parts of their community because of their affiliation. Any negative consequences of that affiliation, if they outweighed the positive, may have functioned as a deterrent to joining a gang. However, few aversive consequences existed. I knew young women at Medgar High whose boyfriends were in prison. This was simply a fact of life in Watts, and little if any stigma was attached to having a boyfriend who was incarcerated. Gang members in Watts who did serve time experienced an increased prestige when they returned to their community. Those who were killed in a gang-related confrontation achieved a form of immortality and were revered by the other gang members, their "homeboys," becoming a part of the legend of the gang.

Reporting of gang-related crimes was minimal in Watts and South-Central Los Angeles. Those who stand up to a gang may be threatened, beaten, or even killed, so they will report gang-related incidents only in anonymity. Thus, because of the lack of evidence or the intimidation of witnesses, few gang members are actually convicted.[11] Since people were afraid of reprisal, they often failed to report gang-related incidents to the police, and gang members were able to continue to operate with impunity.

An intimidated community can maintain the delinquent behaviors that are contributing to its destruction by ignoring them out of fear of reprisal or by accommodating to them. For example, because of the high theft rate in the community, families I knew disconnected not only their car radios but also their car batteries at night, and they took them into their homes for safekeeping. Some of my students had absences from school caused by a need to house-sit. Their families always left at least one person in the house to protect their belongings. If the parent had to take a younger child to the doctor, for instance, the older child would have to stay home because the family would not leave the house unattended for fear of gang-related theft. In this way, threatening situations were accommodated and became just another aspect of people's daily life.

In the late 1980s, the Los Angeles Police Department (LAPD) began "Operation Hammer," a series of antigang sweeps in high-crime neighborhoods designed to be a show of force and police strength to the gangs. Individuals wearing gang-related clothing such as "rags" and caps, showing particular colors, or throwing gang signs were the ostensible target of the sweeps. They were stopped, questioned, and arrested in an attempt to curb parole and curfew violations as a first step in reducing gang activities. Paradoxically, the sweeps may have strengthened gang affiliation and the prestige of those individuals arrested. Young men in Watts were arrested during the sweeps because of their appearance, young men who had nothing to do with gangs but simply happened to have the wrong skin color and to be in the wrong place at the wrong time, which is to say that they were young men of color in Watts when the police were looking for individuals to arrest. I found it both revealing and disturbing that some of my students called the LAPD "the biggest gang in L.A."

Policies of arresting suspected wrongdoers, including gang members, on the basis of their skin color, their manner of dress, or their hair style violated their civil liberties and sent a strong racist and classist message to the young people I knew in Watts. The sense of impotence and powerlessness, clearly widespread within the African American male population in Watts, only increased with such policies. The resultant rage may be said to be one of the biggest killers of African American males. The young men who joined gangs in Watts often turned their rage on one another rather than on the society which created the conditions in which social justice was dormant.

Incidents like the arrests during "Operation Hammer" were common and occurred before and after the initiation of the police sweeps. My students reported that they were routinely stopped and harassed by the police. A typical example occurred when a student of mine named Marcus, a seventeen-year-old African American, was arrested on his front porch. He had been talking to his mother in the kitchen when they heard noises outside. He walked out his door and was arrested because he looked like the suspect for whom the police were searching. "Looked like" all too often translated to being tall, male, and African American.

In fact, I learned about the deceptive nature of appearances early on in Watts in an incident which was both personally enlightening and humbling. As I walked down the street to the elementary school one day early in my second year at Medgar High, I noticed a large group of young men walking toward me, dressed in standard gangbanger attire. Although I had been given a walkie-talkie to carry on my frequent trips back and forth to the elementary school to drop off and pick up my high school students who worked there with the younger children, I felt foolish using it for more than reporting my arrival at or departure from either school. As the group of young men drew closer, I forced myself to keep walking and to refrain from crossing the street, although I was very nervous. When they drew up in front of me, I gasped as one young man separated himself from the group and launched himself at me. He threw his arms around my neck, and yelled, "Dr. Stamnes! How you doing?!" In an instant, this frightening group of "gangbangers" was transformed into a group of laughing kids, one of whom had been a favored student of mine the previous year. Mingled with my relief was a profound sense of shame that I too had not seen beyond appearances. This incident raised a perplexing question for me of how we can teach ourselves to look beyond exterior messages to the person inside and cemented in me the realization that we have to put a human face on the gangbanger, the adolescent mother, and the person living in poverty because it is only then that we will begin to deal with people as individuals rather than as stereotypes, statistics, or media images.

Such incidents of being judged on appearance occurred with adults as well as adolescents. An African American man whom I knew in the community was followed by the police as he drove, dressed in his umpire's uniform, to umpire a Little League baseball game. After following him for blocks, the police finally pulled him over in a shopping center parking lot. He was told to get out of the car, put his hands on the hood, put his feet back, and spread them apart. He escaped being arrested only because an officer whom he knew came onto the scene and was able to vouch for his identity. They stopped him because he was an African American man driving what was perceived to be a "nice" car, the assumption being that the car must have been stolen. He was badly shaken by the experience because he realized that he was still vulnerable, that having entered into middle-class status by hard work did not protect him. In the final analysis, he was suspect because of the color of his skin. He said to me, "Don't you see? This wouldn't have happened to you. It happened to me solely because I'm a black man."

Racism is often thought of as having been a problem of the 1960s. However, it was never resolved and is, if anything, only looming larger in U.S. society as a factor in the determination of poor life options, particularly for African American males in Watts and other inner-city communities. The racism within the society which relegates, for example, the bottom-rung jobs to people of color, who are then the first to be laid off, only contributes to the pervasive lack of options for young people of color.

The young in this country often are shown role models from popular culture who behave violently. Many children are given war toys with which to play and watch violent programs on television, imbibing such messages as violence is an acceptable method of achieving a desired end. They are socialized to believe that boys should be tough and physical. The messages from society are powerful, and it takes sophisticated cognitive maneuvering and critical thinking skills to untangle the hidden agenda. Many young people I knew in Watts were not able to do this, and they seemed to become inured to acts of violence. Their role models were even more potent and potentially destructive when they were violent family members, such as parents or older siblings. Children in Watts whose parents were involved in gangs played at being gang members in the same way their agemates in suburbia might play at being a teacher or a doctor or a parent.

Those students I knew who had a positive and involved male role model in the home seemed to be less likely to join a gang. Victor, a student I knew throughout my time in Watts, was a prime example. His father had raised him and his siblings, worked full-time, was a practicing Muslim, and strongly advocated nonviolence to his son. This man provided an effective role model for Victor, who managed not only to steer clear of gang involvement himself but also helped to positively influence his peers to resist gangs. As a peer counselor in the program I ran at Medgar High, he was a powerful advocate for nonviolence to the younger boys at the school who sought help regarding intimidation by local gangs.

Parenting styles, many of which are culturally determined, have an effect on the young. Within African American culture, parenting styles are largely dominated by a matriarchal structure and tend to imbue female offspring with a value and a role model for being the responsible caregiver. Male offspring are often tended to and taken care of by the females in the family and may lack viable same-sex role models for being active, responsible caregivers in a family setting. In Watts, a lack of expectations for their success, starting at the family level and spreading to the school and community and out to society at large, helped to create a group of adolescent males who often felt lost and without purpose within society. This was the message which was consistently presented to them and which caused them to be candidates for affiliation with a gang.

For some young people, the gang provided a much-needed sense of family. Family life was a factor in gang involvement or rejection. A family that is loving and supportive helps to reduce violence,[12] just as an abusive one can promote it. Of the female gang members I knew in Watts, many had dysfunctional home lives. They created a girls' set or subgroup of a gang, affiliated with a particular boys' set, which appeared to be a viable means of creating the family structure so many of the students lacked. They exhibited closeness, with older members taking care of and nurturing the younger ones.

So often in explanations of the rationale behind gang membership the need to belong is overlooked. One former gang member explained it this way: "What I think is formulating here is that human nature wants to be accepted. A human being gives less of a damn what he is accepted into. At that age—eleven to seventeen—all kids want to belong. They are un-people."[13] Gang members in the inner city saw gang involvement as an inner city version of their white, wealthier peers' affiliations: "Say, we're white and we're rich. We're in high school and we been buddies since grammar school. And we all decide to go to the same college. Well, *we* all on the same street, all those years, and we all just decide to—," another gang member finishes his statement, "—join the gang."[14] These former gang members saw gang membership as a different side of the same coin, the same human need for affiliation and belonging.

For some members I knew, gang life became a trap from which they wanted to escape. However, leaving a gang was more difficult than entering one, for either sex. To enter a gang, a person was "courted in," which usually involved having to fight the other members for a specified amount of time. To leave it, a person had to be "courted out," which involved a free-for-all beating with no time limitation. At times, it also meant death, since leaving a gang was seen as the person withdrawing his loyalty from the other gang members.

Two of the young women I taught who wanted to leave a particular gang decided to simply wait until they graduated, seeing that as a natural break in their affiliation with the gang, a break which avoided the need for a courting-out. However, it was usually not such an easy step, especially for male gang members. One gang member said that he would always be known in the city because of his past involvement, so he felt it was impossible to leave the gang even if he wanted to do so.[15] Affiliation with a particular gang was often seen as a lifetime commitment, and giving up one's life for the gang was considered the ultimate act of loyalty. It revolved around the concepts of turf and family, as mentioned in the beginning of this chapter. The "'hood" was the turf, and the other members of the gang were the family. The code of honor in protecting both was clear and strict: protect your own and avenge any harm to a comember. The lack of opportunity in Watts created an isolated and encapsulated world, the boundaries of which were the neighborhood or "'hood" in which one lived.

The young men I knew in Watts who were unaffiliated with a gang were under tremendous pressure to join one. Gang members verbally assaulted them with "Where you from, man?" which was, in the dialect, asking what was one's gang affiliation. Young men who were not affiliated with a gang would reply, "I ain't from nowhere, man." Although the translation of this was that the person did not have a gang affiliation, the literal version seemed a stark truth, a poignant comment on life in Watts.

Victor, with whom I have kept in close contact since I left Watts, recently told me about consistently being harassed by gang members as he walked on the street. He said that even "little kids, like junior high kids that don't come up to my shoulder," stopped him and demanded to know where he "was from." He batted the little ones out of his way as long as they did not have a weapon. He ran from the older ones, scaling walls and ducking into stores to escape them. A year ago, he called and told me he had been shot at from close range. Horrified, I asked him what he had done, and he laughed out loud and said, "You crazy? I ran as fast as I could!"

The pressure to join a gang often took the form of violence. Some students who were tired of being intimidated joined a gang for protection. I knew parents in Watts who decided to send their sons to live with relatives in another city or state to protect them from the pressure to join a gang and the associated violence. To most, however, this was a luxury that was dreamed about but inaccessible. I lost some of the most promising young men from my programs because of gang intimidation which caused the students to be moved to another school for their own protection.

It is important to note that children raised within the same environment can take divergent paths: of the students I knew Watts, many of whom grew up together in the same neighborhood and attended the same school, some joined gangs and some did not. Those who did not become involved in gang activity had certain behaviors in common: being involved in nongang activities, wearing nongang-related apparel, befriending people from all groups, and avoiding potential trouble.[16]

Some of the students at Medgar High in Watts who were involved in my peer counseling and future teacher programs were able to strengthen their self-esteem by helping others, teaching and tutoring, assisting the elderly, making lunches for the homeless, listening to someone in trouble, or welcoming a new student, to name a few of their activities. They created a sense of extended family within each group and provided a powerful support network for one another. Some reported that they were careful to dress in a way which could not be construed as related to any gang faction, wearing little jewelry so as to not attract the attention of gang members or others who might be interested in stealing it. They tried to be friendly to everyone. When they were attacked, they usually fought back, but they were adept at talking their way out of difficult situations because of their communications and conflict management skills. Such behaviors helped them to resist gang affiliation and conflicts. Further, active participation in such extracurricular programs as athletics, music, art, dance, tutoring, and drama provided some young people at Medgar High with the needed peer support network and access to caring adults which may have helped them resist the recruiting advances of gang members.

However, my students were not always successful in avoiding entanglements with gang members. One Future Teacher was brutally beaten unconscious on a Saturday afternoon as he waited for a bus in front of the school. His attackers were a group of gang members who came up behind him as he sat in the bus shelter in front of the high school and beat him with a pipe. He had just spent the day taking a group of small children on a field trip.

As a teacher, I did not feel particularly threatened by gang members; they were not interested in me. My relations with my students who were involved in gangs were warm and affectionate. One student, however, did threaten me, finally forcing me to realize that I too was not immune. I wrote in my journal on September 17, 1989:

> I've met a kid, Antonio, who claims to be involved with the "Mexican Mafia," says he is selling large amounts of coke [cocaine] and heroin, and tells me he wants to stop but cannot

because of his Mafia connections. I believe this is all fiction designed to impress and lure back his girlfriend, an ex-student/ current counselee of mine. However, he has obliquely referred to killing people, and his girlfriend told me Friday that when she first encouraged him to confide in me, he said he'd have to kill me if he did. I took this news with barely a twitch. However, later, it wore away at me, and I found myself feeling vulnerable and insecure.

It is hard to confess such fears. I believe in what I do, but I am not immune to the elements of insanity which invade parts of the community in which I work. I feel myself at risk, in danger. The rational part of me does not give credence to such thoughts, such rumblings of fear. I am not courageous. I am afraid, but I feel I must find the guts each day to go and do what the kids count on me to do: no miracles, just a bit of love. Still, one does not know the irrationality of a person who is unstable, and I think Antonio is unstable. And I am not invincible. This kid could attack me simply to try to prove that his story is real, and if it is real, it is even more frightening. Amazing: It's only the second week of school.

My other kids are mostly gems, so lovely and energetic that I move at the speed of light to give them all I have. I so love to teach. I just think I'd feel a lot better about it if I weren't afraid of being killed.

Two years after leaving Watts, I finally was able to see the macabre, and wholly unintentional, humor in this passage. At the time, it seemed like just another difficulty to overcome in a normal day as a teacher in Watts. The experience itself helped me gain insight into the effects of the intimidation which is the daily fare of many people who live in Watts and other inner-city communities.

The element most lacking in Watts was hope. One young gang member who was asked what he thought he would be doing in ten years replied that he didn't think he would be alive in ten years.[17] He had little reason to invest in a future he did not envision and for which he had no hope. This lack of hope was a reasonable response to the numbing statistics illustrative of the odds for a young man in Watts. The male mortality rate in Gambia, India, or El Salvador, among the poorest developing countries in the world, is lower than the mortality rate among African American men, with 19 percent of the deaths of African American males due to homicide.[18] Of the young African American men who are living in this country, approximately 30 percent are under court control, either in prison or on probation. In the United States, homicide is the leading cause of death for all African American fifteen- to twenty-four-year-old males, for whom the homicide rate is seven times higher than the overall national rate.[19] Young men in Watts saw little reason for hope with the overwhelmingly high rates of unemployment, mortality, and incarceration. These realities pointed to a bleak future.

Young people who have hope are more likely to value life, to invest in it, and to see a point to staying in school or avoiding pregnancy or staying off drugs. The band-aids that social policy makers have attempted to place over the problems of inner-city communities like Watts have not staunched the flow of blood, stopped the killings, or repaired the wounded psyche of many of the people who live there.

This lack of hope, options, and power was addressed in 1965 during the Watts civil unrest. Some people in Watts and other inner-city communities attempted to find a way to regain a sense of control and power over their own lives, although their acts were desperate, destructive, and ineffective. Little has changed in the intervening years, and once again, a sense of powerlessness and anger at the lack of life options pervade the community. Within the Watts community, that which was absent is telling: opportunities, jobs, high-quality education, affordable and decent housing, and viable policies for socioeconomic change. Politicians and social policy makers have ignored the long-term poor in Watts and other inner-city communities. Society has inflicted upon residents of Watts and other inner cities inferior education with an almost 50 percent attrition rate, dreadfully limited employment opportunities, and substandard housing in segregated communities, refusing to address the issues of job training, drug rehabilitation, and empowerment.

After the civil unrest in Watts in 1965, a master plan called the 25 Year Plan was created as a blueprint for rebuilding the inner city. Few of the proposed changes have been carried out. It is telling that the 1990s brought the building of two new county jails and a prison in Los Angeles. The hopes of the late 1960s and 1970s have shifted from proactive plans for rebuilding the inner city and offering real assistance to people within the community to reactive plans of building new jails and prisons in which to incarcerate its residents.

Inequities within the social structure have caused stressors which may have contributed to crime. Material resources are not equally distributed in the United States, and many of the crimes committed by the poor are economic crimes. As Ramsey Clark stated,

> For the maturing youth, poverty forges values that often lead to violence. No decent home, no family, a relative afflicted with alcoholism and idleness, school drop-out, no jobs, no money, no organized activity or recreation, nothing to do, gangs seeking some release from miserable circumstances, success seen in gambling, drugs, and prostitution, the elderly, weak and sick left in their midst for want of love, all these and more make up that period when personal choices being made at 10 to 20 years of age are likely to lead to violence. It often does.[20]

Thus, the sheer fact of living in poverty, a form of societal violence, can promote acts of individual violence.

In response to these conditions, some of the young have created their own form of power and have demanded not to be ignored. People have begun to pay attention as the homicide tally inexorably rises. The saddest aspect to me as I taught in Watts was that the anger that some of these young people felt was not directed outward to changing the inequities in the social system but inward to killing their peers, those mired in the same dire circumstances, creating what seemed at times like an endless tally of killings and retribution. The retribution was often blind, without a particular object, based upon the rule of a life for a life. It did not seem to matter whose life was taken in retaliation as long as one was taken. A drive-by shooting in retaliation for the killing of a fellow gang member did not discriminate between the Crip or the Blood standing on the corner and the toddler playing near him.

In the United States, we currently have over 1 million people incarcerated in the nation's jails and prisons. We continue to arrest people and to build more prisons in which to incarcerate them, preferring to spend our dollars in a reactive way by housing people in prison cells as they grow up rather than in a proactive way by educating them in classrooms when they are young. It would be much more efficacious to begin to build hope through equitable education, job training, job opportunities, improved housing, and better health care. High-quality and progressive education and values clarification beginning with the young would be a starting point in dealing with the upsurge of racism, acts of racial violence, and intolerance. Bringing businesses back into the Watts community along with government-funded projects to create jobs to rebuild the urban infrastructure would help to provide a more stable economic base and increase employment. If such proactive measures leading to genuine improvements were made in Watts and other inner-city communities in the United States, young people of color might be more willing to invest in life rather than leave the choice between life and death to the squeeze of a trigger from a car window.

CHAPTER 4

Substance Abuse

The effects of substance abuse seemed to touch most of the families I knew in Watts, either directly or indirectly. Within my peer counseling classes, we discussed the use and abuse of alcohol and other drugs. Inevitably when the topic was introduced, students began to volunteer that they had a primary person in their lives—parent, sibling, relative, or friend—for whom alcohol or other drugs were a problem. This revelation was usually followed by tears brought on by their feelings of helplessness in trying to stop what they saw as destructive behavior. Most of the students in each class over the years knew at least one person involved in substance abuse. The use and abuse of alcohol and other drugs in Watts are the subject of this chapter, with a special focus on the reasons for and the consequences of such abuse for adolescents and adults.

Obviously, people drink alcohol and take drugs for a variety of reasons. The reasons cut across class and ethnic boundaries and include, for example, the need to relieve tension, deal with loneliness or depression, or seek relief from frustration and anxiety. Sometimes a temporary difficult event triggers increased drug use, which may then continue even after the situation is resolved.[1] In the community surrounding Medgar High, a dangerous combination existed of readily available drug supplies and stressful and often despair-laden living conditions. An early morning drive along 103rd Street in Watts by the government housing projects near the school revealed people already drinking out of bottles nestled in brown paper bags. My students reported being able to find everything from marijuana to heroin by contacting students they knew on campus. One addicted student said she felt that if she sat in her house "with the doors locked and all the windows barred, the drugs would still get in."

Young people I knew in Watts used alcohol and other drugs partly because of the feelings of increased well being, power, and maturity they associated with such usage. Students said that using alcohol and other drugs made them feel "big and important," "more relaxed," and "grown up." Adolescence was often a time of limbo for many of my students, the in-between time in which they were neither children nor adults. Further exacerbating this sense of being caught between childhood and adulthood was the fact that so few rites of passage into adulthood existed for them. Without a true rite of passage, they sometimes adopted what they perceived as uniquely adult behaviors, such as drinking alcohol, taking drugs, smoking cigarettes, and having sexual intercourse. Experimentation with these activities seemed to signify their passage into adulthood, a fairly common reaction to adolescence.[2] The students I knew who were participating in these activities said that it made them feel more like adults.

Even some of my youngest students saw alcohol in particular as helping them feel better and in making them feel more adult. Children develop expectancies related to alcohol use at an early age, before they actually have experiences with alcohol. In short, they begin to perceive that alcohol produces certain states that seem attractive and desirable. They expect that it will reduce physical tension and cause an increase in personal power or an enhancement of pleasure.[3] These expectancies become clearer with the actual use of alcohol.[4] Indeed, my students seemed to expect a series of positive effects from alcohol long before they began to use it. Students at Medgar High reported that they had heard or observed that alcohol helped people to relax, to feel better, and to feel happy even when life was problematic. "It helps you cope," they said.

Peer pressure played a large role in determining alcohol and other drug usage. Students I knew at Medgar High reported that they found it difficult to refuse to use alcohol or other drugs when asked to by their friends because they were then often ostracized for not using them. In the peer counseling classes, students talked about how they felt when they gave in to pressure to follow the crowd and drink or use drugs, frankly discussing their feelings about being under the influence of these substances. Older students in my programs often served as role models for the ninth- and tenth-grade students, clearly explaining the merits of abstinence and moderation. Younger students could understand the reasons to stay away from alcohol and other drugs, but they had difficulty translating knowledge into action. Here again, older students were able to assist by showing them how to practice moderation and abstinence through role plays and strong and assertive responses to pressure lines from peers. Showing younger students how to respond when pressured was crucial in helping them translate their desires to be moderate or abstemious into action.

Diverse factors affected the degree of drug use of students at Medgar High, including parenting style and parental drug use. In one study, mothers using drugs reported that they had more difficulty in controlling their children than nonusing mothers. This is significant, since those children who are deemed to have problems in conduct as youngsters may also be those who are most likely to use drugs themselves and become involved in delinquent activities in adolescence.[5] Indeed, the frequent use of drugs was found to have a significant relationship to incidents of both minor and violent delinquency among Mexican American, African American, and white male adolescents.[6] Delinquency and drugs were common bedfellows among the addicted young people I knew and among those abusing drugs.

Researchers posit several reasons for the use of illegal drugs. As pointed out earlier, drug use was tied to peer acceptance. In some cases, young people turned to drugs to solicit attention from parents who were abusive or neglectful. As with some suicide gestures, the use of drugs was aimed at calling attention to problems that the young people felt unable to articulate. If parents or caregivers were unresponsive, this reinforced the adolescents' drug use by leading them to conclude that it did not matter what they did, since they perceived that no one cared about them. Such increased use of drugs is one warning sign of possible suicide risk, one I took quite seriously. For some of my students, drugs provided a means of escaping a painful world of despair and a sense of failure.

Some of the students I knew who were addicted and were attempting to overcome their addictions said that although they knew that their similarly addicted friends were the last people with whom they should spend time, they did not know how to break the connection. Until they were able to do so, some continued to use drugs with them to keep from "hurting their feelings." Part of the difficulty in overcoming their addiction was in the social network of people with whom they abused drugs. Giving up the drug meant giving up the people associated with the drug, and this amounted to letting go of an entire network of friends. They revealed that whereas it was difficult enough to overcome an addiction, they found it extremely painful to simultaneously lose those people who had constituted their friends and support system, no matter how destructive they were. However, continued association with friends who were using drugs made it extraordinarily difficult for them to stop using.

The issue of substance abuse at Medgar High had two facets: the drug use of parents, caregivers, or significant others and that of the students themselves. Adults and late adolescents in Watts who were locked into joblessness, were lacking in skills, were receiving welfare, and had little to do that was productive to occupy their time were at increased risk for becoming involved in substance abuse. In some families in Watts, the parents' dreams for their own lives had remained unfulfilled, and they at times turned to alcohol or other drugs to attempt to ease the burden. Women who had married young, had begun childbearing early, had limited interactions outside the home, had little formal education, had few job skills, and were dependent upon the men in their lives for financial support at times became completely disillusioned with their lives and began to use alcohol or other drugs. Men or women who had started life with dreams of what they would accomplish only to remain in low-paying jobs with no chance of advancement or to remain chronically unemployed or underemployed were similarly at risk. Aracely's father was an example of the failed dreams and disillusionment which resulted in binges of drinking that eventually came close to costing him his job. Within some single-parent households, the burden of child rearing and providing for the family caused stress beyond what people felt they could endure, and so they succumbed to alcohol or other drugs as a way of escaping.

In Watts, as in other deindustrialized inner cities, it was difficult to become self-supporting after having received government assistance. Particularly in single-parent families in which there were several small children and an absence of extended family who could share the child care responsibilities, the difficulties at times seemed insurmountable. To obtain employment required that people had child care in order to leave home and go to work. Child care was usually expensive. Consequently, it often ended up being more costly to work than to remain on government assistance and stay at home. In addition, taking what were often low-paying jobs posed further burdens to the family when the job did not provide medical coverage and the family stood to lose the medical coverage provided under federal assistance. I observed

families in Watts in which such a forced choice at times contributed to the despair that started family members on the road to
substance abuse.

Tobacco, alcohol, marijuana, and cocaine, among other
drugs, were readily available in Watts. Crack, a derivative of
cocaine and highly addictive, was also easy to obtain. At prices
ranging from $3.00 to $5.00 a vial, it was an inexpensive high and
a relatively affordable road to possible addiction. In the late
1980s, I began to hear about "ice" (smoked methamphetamine),
which had become available on the street, causing concern among
law enforcement officials, drug rehabilitation counselors, and
educators because it was considered to be even more addictive
than crack and could cause unpredictable and often violent behaviors. The problem was further exacerbated by the fact that it was
difficult to treat people who were abusing such drugs as crack and
ice because these were relatively new drugs, and not much was
known about the consequences of prolonged usage, long-term
health risks, fetal development risks, behavioral changes, and
child development consequences of fetal exposure.

In addition to street drugs, household products were also used
in Watts for their intoxicating effects. These products had the
desirable attributes of being easily available, legal to possess, and
inexpensive. Further, they provided a "quick high"; that is, they
rapidly induced an altered state of consciousness. Such products
as airplane glue, lacquer thinner, fingernail polish remover, model
cement, lighter fluid, and rubber cement are solvents which users
sniffed or inhaled, the majority of users being young and under-
privileged.[7] Although such common products provided a high,
they also increased the probability of violent activity and were
potentially lethal.

Phencyclidine, also known as PCP and angel dust, is a psyche-
delic that was common in Watts. One of my students, Carla, a
nineteen-year-old high school senior and mother, was a long-term
PCP user, although she did not reveal this until her senior year.
She hesitated to confide in an adult at the school because she was
afraid of losing her son and concerned that the teachers to whom
she was close would think less of her. She finally did ask for help
when the severity of her problem made her realize that she ran a
very high risk of having her child removed from her care. The
escalation of drug use by parents like Carla brought to the fore
thorny issues of child welfare and child protection in a society in

which the rights of family have remained relatively sacrosanct; that is, who decides when an addicted parent is incapable of sustaining a family? Certainly, Carla had good reason to fear that her drug use might cause her to lose her son. Her son, however, was the one positive aspect of her life, and her feelings for him kept her from completely giving up and losing herself in her addiction.

One of the major problems I encountered in trying to help someone who had decided to try to overcome dependence on drugs was that many of the treatment programs had a limited number of spaces. In addition, the funds for drug abuse treatment had been severely reduced so that treatment on demand was simply not available. When students I knew were attempting to overcome an addiction, treatment on demand was essential in order to capitalize on their commitment to change their lives. A promise to be wait-listed for treatment which would begin in a month or two or six was tantamount to no treatment at all. My students who were abusing drugs and who were wait-listed for treatment found that their will to change their lives deteriorated as they experienced cravings for the drug, were confronted with availability of the drug, and were pressured by peers to continue using. Thus, a new cycle of abuse began while they were waiting for treatment which often caused them to despair of ever conquering their addiction. Some students were no longer committed to changing their lives by the time treatment possibilities were available.

As with so many problems in contemporary society in the United States, the school is the level at which intervention begins when students need assistance which is unavailable elsewhere, and frequently the initiator of this intervention is the classroom teacher. When teachers identify students who are abusing drugs, they can refer them to the nurse or the school psychologist. At Medgar High, however, the sheer number of troubled students who were facing a multitude of problems was so overwhelming that classroom teachers who cared about their students would often intervene on their behalf. I kept comprehensive referral information on agencies in Los Angeles so that I could refer students for help in cases of, for example, drug addiction, family alcoholism, sexual abuse, and pregnancy. For those students who wanted treatment for an alcohol- or drug-related problem, I made the initial telephone calls, arranged appointments, talked with therapists, and acted as a liaison between the students and the prospective treatment providers. Without such intervention and assistance, the students in all probability would not have received help because they lacked knowledge about local resources, were inexperienced with bureaucracy, and were afraid of confronting their problems and of dealing with authority figures.

I intervened in this fashion for Carla, the young woman using PCP, and sought the assistance of several colleagues in an attempt to arrange a placement in a residential drug treatment facility for her. She was registered in an outpatient treatment facility as an interim measure until a placement became available for her at a residential treatment program for which she was wait-listed. However, the outpatient treatment was not effective for her because of the severity of her addiction, and she stopped attending. In her desperation, she began using again when friends urged her to do so and supplied her with some PCP. One morning, she dropped off her little boy at the Infant Care Center at Medgar High prior to using the drug, then came to school, barricading herself in my office while I was at a local elementary school with a group of my Future Teachers. She was clearly high. She cried and screamed at the collection of administrators, police, and paramedics who had gathered to help her, holding them at bay at my office door. By the time a staff member found me returning with my students from the elementary school, Carla had been crying for me for almost an hour.

As I walked through my classroom to the door of my office, the paramedics warned me that she could be violent. In my office, I saw Carla, curled in a ball on the floor behind my desk. She was hugging herself tightly, and her face was painted by the streaks of tears and mascara smeared across her cheeks. She was moaning my name and rocking herself, telling the men at the door to stay away. When she heard me say her name, she looked up in anguish and held out her arms like a small child wanting to be picked up. I went in and sat on the floor with her and held and rocked her while she cried. The police backed away from the door so that I could quiet her. She kept saying over and over, "You have to help me. No one will help me. You have to help me." When she was calm enough to allow the paramedics to come in and check her vital signs, we convinced her to go with me in the ambulance to the hospital, where she was admitted into the emergency room. Once she was placed in a bed, she vacillated at a dizzying speed between tears and laughter, pessimism and optimism.

Carla came to school several days later, seemingly forgetting the experience in my office and our long day together at the hospital. She was angry and belligerent, demanding placement at a treatment facility that was residential rather than outpatient. One of the staff members in the school-based health clinic found a place that would take her immediately for two weeks, although she needed months rather than weeks of treatment. She was not satisfied with this because it conflicted with the date of her graduation from Medgar High. She then became even more belligerent, saying that they had to let her out for graduation, which was scheduled to occur in a little over a week. Watching the mercurial changes in her behavior made it distressingly obvious how desperately she needed professional help.

Carla checked into the treatment center and then checked out early to attend graduation. She continued to need help, and in fact I suspected with some chagrin that she had been using prior to the graduation ceremony. Carla needed empathy and enlightened, effective assistance. She was stuck inside an addiction, battling to fulfill her responsibilities toward her son, convinced at nineteen that she was a failure in life. Just as membership in a gang can be a reaction to feelings of isolation and hopelessness, so can immersion in alcohol and other drugs. The all-too-frequent cycle of abusive families, early childbearing, poor education, and lack of job skills and future prospects can be a direct path to substance abuse.

For people involved with Carla as friends or caregivers, as with other similarly addicted people, the task was a trying one. Carla exhibited behaviors while under the influence of which she had no recollection when she was "straight," and this was a common occurrence. The addicted father of Sam, one of my students, stole all of his son's money to buy more drugs. Sam told me of the theft of his entire savings, shrugging his shoulders and saying, "It's happened before. He doesn't even remember he did it."

The need for the drug became so powerful that people at times lost all track of their lives. My students told stories of drug-addicted relatives who were literally wasting away to living skeletons before their eyes. They knew young women, called "strawberries" in the street vernacular at that time, who traded sex for drugs. Living in such close proximity to crack houses and drug dealers, my students were matter-of-fact about the violence and decay which permeated the neighborhood. They spoke of "white people in fancy cars, you know, like BMWs" who came into the neighborhood to make a drug buy, principally buying cocaine. Small children directed these people to the street where they could pull over to the curb and buy what they wanted as easily as buying a hamburger from a fast-food restaurant. Many of my students registered anger at this, saying that poor people in the inner city were being blamed for the drug problem but that poor people didn't have money to buy expensive "designer drugs" like cocaine; they were too busy trying to survive. These young people at Medgar High felt that it was the more affluent people who came into the neighborhood to buy drugs who perpetuated the drug trade that was so destructive to the community and the people who lived there.

Victor, a student of mine mentioned earlier, spoke of a woman who lived near him who was so absorbed in her own addiction that she neglected her small son. The child was "raggedy," Victor said, needing a bath and clean clothes. At one point, Victor became so concerned that the child was being neglected that he took him home to feed him. Other students spoke of siblings who stole money and possessions from the family in order to support their addiction. As one girl said, "There's nothing they won't do—steal, lie, cheat. You can't trust them." Yet even with this clear-eyed assessment of the behaviors of the addicted people in their lives, my students retained a sense of sympathy for their sufferings even as they experienced pain at their betrayals.

Students in the peer counseling classes realized they did not have the expertise needed to help the addicted people in their lives make changes to break their addiction. They saw that professional help was needed. However, they learned and practiced methods of being loving and supportive without becoming a party to the addiction and then used the methods with their loved ones who were using and abusing drugs. Further, they learned about the local substance abuse resources in the community so they could refer people when they decided they needed and wanted help. Finally, they shared knowledge of the incredible pervasiveness of drugs and the epidemic level of violence surrounding them in their community, and thus were able to lend support to one another as they coped with the personal and communal tragedy and grief related to drugs.

Necessary measures to combat the growing drug problem in Watts and other inner-city communities include early educational intervention (starting at the elementary school level), free access to clear information about substance abuse, peer counseling which allows children and adolescents to influence and educate their peers, and treatment upon demand for those who are ready to confront and attempt to overcome their drug dependency. However, the problems go much deeper than this surface-level analysis, and so must the solutions. Parents need to be supported within such high-risk communities through parenting classes focusing on parenting skills specifically dealing with preadolescents and adolescents, substance abuse risks and signs, neighborhood antidrug watch activities, and early identification of at-risk children. After-school programs and community activities need to be instituted so that children and adolescents have viable alternatives to spending time on the streets. Tutoring services need to be offered to those who need them. A culturally based program of ethnocultural intervention may further reduce the incidence of drug use among high-risk minority youths.[8]

Beyond these community-based solutions, changes on a societal level must be accomplished. Drug sales activities are often alluring because they provide quick money in large sums. Estimates of the spoils of individual drug earnings run from $200 to $3,000 per day; yet even using the low-end figure and factoring in the irregularity of the work, dealers could earn $2,000 per month, an almost 400 percent increase over minimum wage earnings.[9] This becomes a powerful incentive to deal drugs rather than participate in scarce mainstream, legal employment where the pay is often at the level of the minimum wage. Thus, the introduction of more minimum wage jobs into the community, jobs which offer life below the poverty line, is not the answer. People in Watts need training for employment which will earn them a living wage, one which will enable them to support their families. As long as society does not provide opportunities to inner-city youth which can realistically compete with those provided by the drug trade, such activities as dealing drugs will continue to thrive.

A frequently asked question is how the drugs arrive in Watts and other inner-city communities in the first place. They are not grown or produced in the community, yet they are omnipresent. It stretches credulity to believe that the pipeline of drugs into this country cannot be turned off. Gangs control drugs sales in Watts, and they are one of the main reasons for the increased violence in the community as different factions compete for turf and shares of the drug market. Some gang members in Watts maintained that if the supply of drugs and weapons were halted, violent gang activity would immediately decrease. Focus on the relatively small-time dealers in communities like Watts in lieu of those who are importing drugs into the country on a massive scale will continue to stop the minor leaks but will do nothing to stop the flood. As long as illegal drugs are available in Watts and the pressing needs of the community are ignored, substance abuse will continue to shatter lives, and the residents of Watts will continue to suffer either as witnesses of the addictions of their loved ones or as victims of substance abuse and addiction, as in the case of Carla, who saw drugs as so inescapable that she felt she had no safe place to hide.

CHAPTER 5

Stress, Education, and the Inner City

During the first few weeks I taught in Watts, I began a unit on para-graph writing with the seniors in the class I taught on basic writing skills. We started off with a group-writing exercise beginning with a brainstorming session from which we developed sentences that were later worked into paragraph form. When I asked the students that morning what they wanted the topic to be, they decided to write about Watts. They called out words and phrases they associated with Watts, and I wrote them on the board. One student mentioned a phrase I could not decipher, and I put it down to the fact that my ear was not yet completely attuned to the students' dialect. I asked several times for the student to repeat what she had said, then turned in some consternation to the other students for assistance. They called out the same phrase, one which I simply could not understand. In exasperation at my own obtuseness, I said, "Spell it." They obliged, after consulting one another on the correct spell-ing, with, "B-A-T-T-E-R-I-N-G R-A-M." "Battering ram?" I asked. In amazement that I did not know the significance of a bat-tering ram in Watts, they proceeded to describe to me how the doors and walls of their houses and the houses of friends, relatives, and neighbors had been pounded in with a battering ram by the police. Eventually, after listening carefully to my students and doing some research, I learned about battering rams, introduced by former LAPD police chief Daryl Gates as a weapon in the so-called drug war. Its ostensible use was to batter in the doors of suspected crack houses. Unfortunately, crack houses are sometimes difficult to dif-ferentiate from family homes. Such was the reality of my students' lives.

Post-traumatic stress disorder (PTSD) is a term most often associated with Vietnam veterans, those who returned to the United States and who suffer as a reaction to the stressor of having been involved in war. PTSD is often described as a normal reac-tion to an abnormal situation; that is, it is normal to have a strong adverse emotional and psychological reaction to such abnormal

101

stresses as extreme violence, injury, and death. However, it is not only war veterans who suffer from PTSD; people, including children, in Watts and other inner-city communities also suffer from this disorder. Theirs is a reaction to the violence which filters from their communities into their lives from both sides of the law.

It is startling to the uninitiated to hear young people talk about violence and death as though they were everyday affairs. In Watts, they *were* an everyday occurrence, and people attempted to cope with the omnipresence of death and violence by constructing various defense mechanisms which helped them continue living on a day-to-day basis. However, these mechanisms were not constructed without a cost to the individual, and it is these costs which will be the subject of this chapter.

Watts is a community where the leading cause of death for African American males is homicide; where the infant mortality rate, the incidence of communicable disease, and the morbidity and mortality rates are the highest in Los Angeles County; and where the rate of immunization and the number of medical doctors per capita are the lowest in the county.[1] Eighty-three percent of the individuals who are treated at the local medical facility, Martin Luther King, Jr., Hospital and Drew Medical Clinic, are trauma cases treated for wounds, mostly caused by guns.[2] During my third year at Medgar High, from January to July of 1989, 237 homicides, 9,068 aggravated assaults, 413 rapes, and 5,864 robberies occurred in South-Central Los Angeles alone.[3] Such a picture does not sound like a community within the United States but rather a sketch of a poor "third world" community to which the foreign policy response of the United States might be to offer aid. Little aid, however, was offered to Watts and other inner-city communities. They were not the forgotten regions of our country; they were simply ignored.

By the 1989–90 academic year, conditions in Watts had barely improved and in some cases had significantly worsened since the so-called Watts riots in August of 1965. Indeed, the conditions were ripe for a second uprising because the ingredients of the first in large measure still remained. Accusations of police brutality, inequitable educational opportunities in de facto segregated schools, low involvement of African Americans and Latinos in community businesses, pervasive joblessness, wretched housing, living conditions well below standards throughout the county, and insufficient medical care and preventive health care were all issues which created the climate into which the Watts civil disturbance exploded in 1965, and these remained the major issues in the early 1990s. The recommendations of the McCone Commission Report in 1965 were still largely unfulfilled. Tensions between community members and the police were high and were further exacerbated by the many complaints of police brutality toward minority residents. Racial tension between the expanding Latino community and the diminishing African American community within Watts was increasing and was mirrored in the neighborhood schools, taking the form of clashes between African American and Latino students at Medgar High at the end of the school year in 1990.

Even during my first year at Medgar High, it was fairly easy to detect an uneasiness between the African American and Latino students. They entered the classroom and sat in self-segregated groups. When I questioned them directly about this, they said they did not sit with one another because they were familiar with members of their "own group" and they lacked information about one another. My students discovered that they held many stereotypical notions which they were able to dispel through discussion and through the establishment of friendships across their previously self-imposed boundaries. This is not to say that prejudice was always conquered in these classes. One young woman, who typified students holding deeply rooted prejudices, said to the class one day as we sat in a circle and discussed issues of ethnicity and race, "I hate Mexicans. I can't help it." The other students asked her to explain her reasons, and she replied, "My grandmother [who raised her] hates Mexicans, so I do too. She says they're coming in here and taking over." The students, disturbed and rather confused by this, asked her what "they" were taking over. She said with some emotion, "This place! Watts! They're taking all the jobs and places to live." With such students, even their increased interactions with students of other races and ethnicities did not succeed in reducing their firmly held prejudices.

Within this environment, children were being born and were growing up bearing the scars of the community's problems, problems of such long standing that they had touched generations who passed along as their legacy the belief that things would never change. Added to this widespread sense of hopelessness was the violence that existed in Watts and other inner-city communities. Drive-by shootings claimed innocent lives weekly. My students complained of having to hit the floor every time they heard a loud noise, even a car backfiring, in case it was a stray bullet that could kill someone sitting at the table eating a meal. Children were afraid to play outside, with good reason: some had been killed on a local school playground. A nearby elementary school sponsored a "grief class" designed to help children learn to cope with the violence and death they continually witnessed.[4]

Medgar High rarely had night dances like other schools in the district because of the danger of being in the neighborhood after dark. Functions at the school were attended by police helicopters hovering overhead. Football games, afternoon dances, and graduations inevitably were accompanied by the drone and buzz of low-flying police helicopters that made the school reminiscent of a war zone. At an outdoor graduation one year, we could not hear the names of the graduates as they were called up to receive their diplomas because of the deafening noise of the police helicopters. It made me wonder once again if the community was being protected or was under siege.

Most of the students I knew in Watts had lost one or more relatives and/or friends to violent deaths. Just bringing up the subject of death often caused a chain-reaction: one student began to talk about having lost someone, and one by one students covered their faces with their hands and began to cry. Although initially mystified by this reaction, I later understood that these students had experienced losses, often caused by violence, which were so numerous that rarely were they able to grieve fully, leaving them with a residue of grief that came to the surface at the first mention of death.

At times, I felt that they had witnessed an unending parade of violence; everyone in my classes had a story to tell when the subject arose. One student had seen her uncle shot in the head in her backyard. Many spoke of gang members running through their yards and apartment buildings, shooting at members of rival gangs, spraying the building and anything in sight with bullets. My students spoke of their fear of being on the street. Girls were frequently knocked down and had their necklaces ripped from their necks. When they wore any jewelry, such as a necklace or a small ring or a bracelet, they hid them as they walked to school so that no one would attempt to steal them. Once at school, they were still not safe. The administration was able to do little to protect them from such attacks. One dean sighed after hearing yet another report of this type of theft and said to the student, "Stop wearing jewelry to school. You're asking for it to be stolen here."

Another student described how he had hidden behind a heavy curtain in his apartment and watched as members of a local gang vandalized his car, banging in the top, stealing the radio, and slashing the tires. He had worked hard bagging groceries at a local market to be able to buy the car and was heartbroken at the senseless destruction. When I asked him if he had called the police, he gave me a "you've got to be kidding" look and said, "What for? They wouldn't come or if they did, they'd take their time and be too late to do anything. What's the point?" There were few happy endings to my students' stories.

One morning as I drove down 103rd Street in Watts on my way to the high school, I came to a police roadblock and was sent on a detour. At the time, it was simply another irritation of city life and the commute to work. I arrived at school and began to hear stories from my students about why the roadblock was in place. The previous evening, a gang member had been shot to death as he used the telephone on 103rd Street. The body had remained where it fell through the morning hours, and elementary, junior high, and senior high school students walked past the body on their way to school. A friend of mine on the faculty started to teach that morning and realized from the looks on her students' faces that something was wrong. The students were in shock, and when they told her what had happened, she set aside her lesson plan and helped them to cope with what they had seen. This is a typical example of the juxtaposition of education in Watts and the real lives of the students we were trying to serve: a teacher stood conjugating verbs at the board while the students sat in shock thinking about the dead body they had to step around on their way to school.

In an attempt to respond to the realities of life in Watts, a psychologist affiliated with the district's suicide prevention program worked with me to help a group of my peer counseling students learn skills to cope with the staggering levels of stress in their lives. When these students were tested on a standard measure of adolescent stress, they scored way off the top of the chart in terms of the current life stress they were experiencing. Many of the students concurrently had experienced the death of a close relative, the death of a close friend, the ending of a relationship, a recent move, a family member involved in substance abuse, and the divorce or separation of their parents or primary caregivers.

Intervention took several forms. Students were encouraged to talk about their lives. They were taught techniques to take stock of the physical manifestations of stress within their bodies. They were given tools to use to help them relax and cope with these physical manifestations of stress, including such techniques as breathing exercises, physical relaxation, visualization, and meditation. The group functioned as a strong support network for the students, providing them not only with close peer support but also with the support of two caring, attentive adults. Students made commitments to the group to use the skills they were learning as they attempted to overcome poor coping skills.

Students involved in the group reported a reduction of perceived manifestations of stress, although the actual stressors in their lives remained the same. They reported that they used the techniques they had learned in the group, and, even a year later when I met with six of the original ten who had been in the group, they reported that they continued to use the techniques when they confronted a stressful situation or became aware through self-inventory techniques that they were experiencing increased physical and emotional stress. In short, they were able to reduce their perceived stress level and use more effective methods of stress management through the information and skills obtained as part of the training program.

Since inner-city youth and African American adolescents in particular are subject to higher blood pressure than their white peers because of the external stressors of poverty, poor living conditions, institutional racism, lack of quality educational and occupational opportunities, and poor medical care,[5] it seems a worthwhile project to include stress management training within the curriculum of inner-city schools. Such early and continuous stress has negative long-term health effects that could be reduced through early intervention.

A major physical stressor in Watts was poor nutrition. Nutrition among low-income families was problematic and caused physical disorders, particularly in the young. To eat healthy meals on a small budget required knowledge of nutrition and cooking skills. Because of their lack of education about healthy and affordable food choices, some families I knew consumed foods that offered little nutrition but were high in fat and calories. Cheeses, fatty meats, and fried foods figured prominently in their diets. My students teased me about eating low-fat yogurt and fruit for lunch and about the fact that I did not eat red meat, something that seemed very strange to them. They said they were "eating like Dr. Stamnes" whenever they had what they considered to be a healthy lunch in lieu of "junk food," and I offered information on nutrition to all students who were interested, although I admit that few were.

Students at Medgar High frequently ate "junk food" for breakfast, nutrition break, and lunch. For some, such consumption of "empty calories" led to weight gain and eventual obesity. Many adolescents in Watts were overweight. I found it pertinent that one study on hypertension among a group of African American women who were college students found that 39 percent of the students were obese.[6] Indeed, obesity is a factor in elevated blood pressure and risk of cerebrovascular disease, the third leading case of death among African Americans.[7] These figures were disturbing in light of the poor nutrition of so many of my students. Victor, for example, at seventeen had a very high cholesterol level which was, according to a doctor who had examined him, directly related to his diet.

Environmental influences had a strong impact on stress levels and hypertension among Watts residents. Such stress-producing incidents as joblessness, inadequate housing, and crime may be precursors of hypertension.[8] Some Watts residents felt that they were not in control of their lives because they were forced to react continually to the stressors in their environment, and this caused great anxiety. They worried about crime, their ability to protect their families, life-threatening situations, confrontations with government bureaucracy, and competition for the scarce jobs and resources available to them. Such long-term anxiety created a health risk, especially when coupled with other potential health hazards such as tobacco use, poor nutrition, obesity, and poor physical fitness.

Adolescent pregnancy, lack of prenatal and postnatal care, and early assumption of family caretaking responsibilities were also stressors in Watts. For families living in poverty, without either employer-based health insurance or the means to afford private insurance, a major illness or accident had a devastating effect on the financial well being of the family. Living in poverty created long-term anxiety as individuals attempted to provide food, shelter, and clothing for their families, living in fear of a catastrophe which could literally force them out onto the streets. The working poor, those living at a subsistence level, were particularly vulnerable to displacement by a catastrophic event such as illness, the loss of a job, or the death of a provider. I knew students whose families lived in this way, one of whom I mentioned earlier, and they found it difficult to concentrate on academics when they were worried about whether or not they would soon be homeless.

The teachers who were involved with students in Watts also experienced significant stress. We often felt we were on the front lines in a war without having been given the weapons to fight the battle. Teachers at Medgar High frequently had inferior textbooks and equipment, were given little or no specialized training for teaching in the inner city, and taught in an environment in which the physical plant (as the buildings are known in educational jargon) was far too often filthy, deteriorating, dilapidated, and depressing.

The women's faculty room at Medgar High had one ancient couch so dirty that most people did not want to sit on it. Its one toilet was often backed up and unusable; several of us calculated one day that it was used by approximately sixty-five women from the administration building, an adjacent building, and guests to the school. The sink did not have hot water, and the window over the toilet was without a window pane throughout most of my time at Medgar High. The tap had been modified so that it did not stay on unless it was held, and the soap container was rarely filled with soap. Toilet paper and paper towels were only occasionally provided. The students' restroom facilities were even worse, so bad, in fact, that I had some students who actually refused to use them. Because of the lack of toilet paper in restrooms for students, I kept a supply of tissues on hand for students to take with them to the bathroom. When even such basic needs were not being met at Medgar High, it was not surprising that the more complex educational needs were also not met. Such conditions contributed to low morale at the school.

My first classroom at the school was on the second floor by the staircase in a building that served as a hangout for those students who had "ditched" class. The stench of urine and feces, mingled with the smell of marijuana and tobacco, were omnipresent to the point that the doors to the classroom could not be left open. One administrator's reaction was to have deodorizers installed in the classroom, which seemed to be akin to society's typical manner of problem resolution for Watts and other inner cities: cover it up.

Ceiling tiles in the hallway had either fallen or were dislodged. Graffiti bloomed all over the walls and the stairwell as various gang members wrote their names and crossed out those of their rivals. A glass insert in a classroom door had a bullet hole in it. Sections of the walls displayed large holes where someone had slammed open a door or kicked or punched in the wall. Fluorescent lights flickered on and off prior to going out completely and remaining out sometimes for the entire year.

In this environment, teachers were asked to teach and students were asked to learn. To both was communicated the message that this school was the "bottom of the barrel" in terms of the district's priorities, that nothing important was expected to happen here. Repetition of such phrases as "I am somebody" was hollow at best when the entire environment provided for learning said that nobody of any importance was being served. Students who noticed flowers being planted and planters being hung at the school right before a visit by Jesse Jackson saw the irony. The planters came down after his visit. The message was clear: Jesse was somebody; they were not. Afterwards, whenever my students saw the planters being hung or saw people planting flowers, they would say with biting irony, "Plants! I wonder who's coming to visit?" They knew such decorations were not for them.

The covert messages, known to educators as the "hidden curriculum," were much stronger than the overt messages constantly given to the student body in the form of mottoes and upbeat sayings. For example, classrooms at the school, except for the new modular or portable units, were not air-conditioned, even though temperatures in Los Angeles hit the nineties and above for weeks at a time. The building in which my classroom was located was next to the administration building. We had no relief from the heat through open doors because I had to keep my doors closed and locked to discourage chaotic interruptions by the students or community members who roamed the halls. Further, I had to keep my windows closed on hot days when the heat inside my room exceeded the temperature outdoors by ten degrees. The reason for keeping the windows closed was simple. A huge, ancient air-conditioning unit was located outside of my classroom, and the noise it made as it operated made it impossible for my students and me to hear one another unless we kept the windows closed. The air-conditioning unit did not serve students in their classrooms. Its function was to air-condition the main office where the principal and secretaries worked.

My students understood the irony implicit in this situation and expressed their cynicism about educational priorities. Mari said, "I thought school was supposed to be a place where students learned. How can we learn when it's too noisy to hear with the windows open and too hot to think with them closed? We are trying to learn. Shouldn't *we* have the air-conditioning if anyone does?" They understood the implied message from the administration that the important work at the school was being accomplished in the office, not in the classrooms.

Teachers also recognized the hidden message that what we were doing at Medgar High was not important. Some felt that their job was just to "baby-sit" the students, because it seemed that little learning was expected to take place. This notion was only reinforced by such situations as being expected to teach a course with insufficient textbooks or textbooks which were well beyond the students' levels of reading and cognitive development. At the start of each semester, some teachers felt completely demoralized when the remedy they were offered for their grossly overcrowded classrooms was simply to be told not to worry because by the second week of the semester many of the students would have stopped coming to school. The implied message was that these students were expendable, and indeed that we counted on them to remove themselves from the educational process. We did not fill out our grade books until the fourth or fifth week of the semester, using temporary roll and grade sheets instead. By that time, many of the students we had officially on our rolls had dropped out, so that of our original class list of, for example, forty students, we ended up with a class of twenty. The school counted on that attrition, and it occurred with disturbing repetition. Although many dedicated teachers did not succumb to this message, some fell prey to cynicism and hopelessness, which they then conveyed to their students.

An additional source of demoralization at the school was the lack of funding sources. At many schools, parents and local businesses often function as supporters of school activities. However, in Watts, the typical family did not have the financial resources to send money to school with their children, and the businesses had long left the community. Thus, it fell to caring teachers to assist students and to procure the supplies needed in the classroom. Teachers at Medgar High often supplemented their classroom supplies out of their own limited financial resources, buying books, magazines, supplies, tissues, and toilet paper for their students. Teachers were a source of funding for clubs, activities, and sporting events. Students and teachers put on car washes and candy and bake sales, held garage sales, and asked for contributions to enable students to attend sports or school events and conferences, to buy uniforms, and to travel to competitions.

Beyond that, some teachers at Medgar High gave to their students in other, more personal ways. They brought them their own children's clothes, cribs, and toys as their children outgrew them for the students to use with their babies. They took students out shopping and purchased clothing for them so they could attend graduation or the prom. They gave them money for food, took them to dinner, spent time with their families, and gave them presents to celebrate their accomplishments. In short, teachers voluntarily gave of their own money and their time to expand the options open to students at Medgar High.

Teachers on the faculty at Medgar High were not united in their approach to inner-city education. Such divisions caused stress among faculty members, for example, between those who wanted to impose strict order on the students and those who opposed draconian measures. At Medgar High, the administrative response to a growing graffiti problem on campus was to institute an unannounced search of all students on campus in an attempt to confiscate any permanent markers that could be used in writing graffiti. The search included body pat-downs for males and purse searches for females. Young women watched as their purses were dumped on desks to reveal even personal items like sanitary napkins and tampons. Young men emptied their pockets and were frisked. Students had their highlighter pens and white correction fluid confiscated, neither of which would make effective tools for graffiti. My students were outraged, saying that they felt violated. Some came to me in tears at what they perceived to be a betrayal by the administration. "They treated us like criminals," they cried.

Whereas some faculty applauded this measure, others of us were outraged, refused to participate, and protested that such actions were a violation of students' rights. This type of philosophical difference among staff members increased the ambient stress levels of teachers as one group fought to control students by keeping them passive and quiescent, and another fought to empower them, arguing that searches without cause further reinforced to our students that they were indeed powerless. Thus, one faction argued for education as a force of social control while another argued for education as a means of empowerment. Until the staff members of inner-city schools like Medgar High are able to reach a consensus regarding the basic educational philosophies and goals of their schools, such difficulties will continue to arise.

As discussed earlier, parents within the community were generally not involved in the education of their children as parents often are in more materially advantaged communities. At other schools in the district, parents were vitally involved in their children's education, for example, sitting in on classes and previewing reading lists, but this level of involvement rarely happened at Medgar High. This lack of parental involvement was a crucial factor in some teachers feeling that they were not accountable for what happened in their classes. Thus, the incidence of racist remarks, sarcastic and caustic comments, and harassment was distressingly high. One substitute teacher, a white man, repeatedly was called back to work at Medgar High even though he was not only tremendously unprofessional but also insulting and racist. I returned from a one-day absence to find that he had been placed in my classroom despite my explicit instructions to the contrary. When I arrived at my classroom, one of my students was in tears, and the rest were furious. They said that this substitute teacher had made numerous racist remarks to them and even instructed one young girl to "get her big black ass over here"; even in the retelling of this incident, she cried. Another teacher referred to students hanging around in the quad area outside of his classroom as "apes in the jungle." Students learned painful messages about adults' perceptions of their worth from such occurrences.

The picture reconstructed here is depressing and true. The remedies to solve the problems inherent in inner-city education must begin with a redefinition of the educational process. Compensatory education fails in accomplishing its goal. One study concluded that compensatory education fails for the same reason compensatory medicine would fail; just as medicine delivers the best in care to those who are seriously ill in the form of intensive care or cardiac care units, so should education deliver the same level of intensive care for those members of society who are disadvantaged and vulnerable.[9]

Thus, the public educational system in this country needs to initiate an "intensive care" program for inner-city education. It should recruit quality teachers, those who have been trained specifically for the unique demands of that environment and who have a broad and fundamental knowledge of and sensitivity to multicultural issues of ethnicity and race, class, religion, and language, to name a few. Indeed, for those who lack contacts or interactions in the inner city, teaching there is tantamount to a cross-cultural experience. Teachers who are new to teaching in that environment need an enlightened interpreter of the culture. Teachers who enter into teaching in the inner city without this assistance may experience just enough of the new culture to reject it because it may seem so foreign or incomprehensible to them. This is the reason behind much of high attrition rate among inner-city educators. Teachers with a long tenure in the inner city would be able to function as "cultural trainers" and would be able to guide the immersion experiences of new teachers, providing them with the knowledge they need to understand the new culture and helping them to interpret their experiences.

Not only do teachers need to understand the microculture that is the inner city, but they also need to be sensitive to linguistic differences that occur within that microculture and advocate for the students' right to their own language or dialect. Often, teachers from the dominant culture enter an inner-city school like Medgar High and proceed to label students' dialects as incorrect or faulty. The model used in this comparison is "standard" English. My philosophy was that the students needed to be encouraged to be multidialectical, to communicate fluently across a variety of situations using the situationally appropriate dialect. Thus, for example, they had one dialect they could use with friends on the street which was absolutely correct within that setting and another they could use in a job interview that might sound quite different from the first. We all speak differently depending on the setting in which we find ourselves. Helping students to be multidialectical rather than burdening them with demeaning and alienating value judgments of correct and incorrect speech creates an inclusive atmosphere in the classroom, a sense of an accepting community.

Training needs to be ongoing to offer teachers up-to-date information on advances in education and to provide them with a forum in which to cope with the stress of teaching in the inner city. These specially trained and selected teachers should be compensated for training for and accepting demanding inner-city job assignments. A broad multicultural perspective needs to be incorporated into the public school curricula; that is, the curricula need not be Eurocentric or male dominated: women's and ethnic and class minorities' contributions to society in the United States need to be presented as an integral part of the coursework.

Students need to be treated equally and equitably, and expectations for all students need to reflect the notion that all students are expected to work up to their potential and that no less will be accepted. Girls need to be encouraged in math and science, and teachers must be educated in how their interactions with girls can curtail girls' motivation and intellectual growth in these areas. Children in Watts, like their agemates elsewhere, came to their first day of kindergarten filled with curiosity and looking excited and full of wonder at the new experience, yet somehow in the process of "being educated," these ingredients so essential to academic success and a love of learning were crippled. Perhaps a strong commitment to excellence by the entire faculty and administrative staff of inner-city schools would help to preserve students' expectations and positive self-esteem, a commitment that would replace the sometimes overtly stated cynicism that currently exists with some faculty members. Parent involvement, another necessary ingredient, needs to be encouraged and facilitated.

For students undergoing the traumas inherent in living in an inner-city community like Watts, peer mentoring programs can be effective in reducing stress and resolving problems. Student counselors in the peer counseling program at Medgar High in Watts were trained in communication and conflict resolution skills. Data collected over the course of one semester with twenty-three peer counselors revealed that they were involved in a total of 506 problem resolution situations at Medgar High, at the elementary school, and within the community. They helped people cope with problems in such areas as school, relationships with parents and peers, sex and pregnancy, suicidal feelings, gang-related activities and violence, death and dying, racial tension, and depression and stress.[10] Thus, these students had a strong and positive impact on their school and community.

Yet even such modifications to the public educational system in the United States might receive much criticism. These modifications require that all educators involved in the process analyze their own perceptions and biases and become educated about cultures and people different from their own. Instructors need education to become truly multicultural, that is, free from a dominant culture bias and contributive to the attainment of a truly pluralistic society of the United States. Finally, educators must deal openly with the stresses of the students who live and the teachers who teach within the inner city, stresses very different from those found in most other schools. Children cannot learn and teachers cannot teach if they are feeling traumatized by the violence, poverty, and fear that often go hand in hand with being in many inner cities in the United States. Until societal conditions improve, and Watts can be considered a safe place to live and work and nurture young people into adulthood, educators need to address the issues implicit in being raised in the inner city, lest we lose the overwhelming majority of yet another generation to hopelessness and despair.

CHAPTER 6

In the Wake of the Uprising

As was mentioned in the introduction, the civil unrest in South-Central Los Angeles in April of 1992 occurred as I was working on one of the later drafts of this book. Indeed, having observed in the 1980s and early 1990s the worsening conditions in South-Central Los Angeles, having researched and written about them, having concluded as I did in earlier chapters that the conditions were distressingly ripe for another uprising like the one in Watts in 1965, my reaction to the anger and violence in South-Central L.A. was one of profound sorrow, made poignant by the lack of shock I experienced. Such an occurrence had been both expected and predicted not only by me but by people within the Watts community who had watched the familiar warning signs mount and who felt anger that apathy toward their plight seemed to be the reigning attitude of a large segment of society. This chapter, written in the wake of the civil unrest, is in essence an addendum, not part of the original design of the book but central to its message. It includes a discussion of the civil unrest and its causal factors, factors which have been discussed at length in earlier chapters.

At 3:15 P.M. on Wednesday, April 29, 1992, a verdict of "not guilty" was returned on ten of the eleven counts against four white Los Angeles Police Department officers charged (in the state trial) in the beating of motorist Rodney King. The four officers were acquitted of the charges stemming from the beating which took place on March 3, 1991, and which was videotaped and later broadcast by a Los Angeles television station on March 4, 1991. The eighty-one seconds of videotaped footage left little doubt in the minds of many people all over the world that Rodney King had been brutally beaten by the police officers.

For many people of color in Los Angeles, this trial represented a real chance for justice. The jury, after being confronted with the graphic, seemingly irrefutable evidence of the videotape, would surely recognize the actions of the officers as police brutality, a first step toward public acknowledgment that such problems do exist, especially for people of color in urban areas like Los Angeles. Although the beating stirred angry reactions in Los Angeles and the United States and around the world, a sense of hope and anticipation for impending justice prevailed. The case seemed so clear; the result seemed inevitable.

To many whites living within the dominant culture, a brutal beating by the police is unfathomable, an occurrence simply not a part of their life experiences. They view the police as the public servants they are mandated and trained to be. However, many African American and Latino residents in South-Central Los Angeles had a perception quite different from this benign one. They viewed the police as an alien occupation force, as harassers and persecutors. To these people, Rodney King's beating at the hands of the LAPD was not an unusual occurrence; such beatings and harassment happen with great regularity. What was unusual was the evidence in the form of the explicit videotaped footage. When the not-guilty verdict was announced, many people felt demoralized, infuriated, and embittered. As more than one African American commented, "What this verdict says is that the life of a black man in this country isn't worth anything."

Rodney King was an African American man and by definition at risk for being abused by police in many communities in this country. He was dark-complected, and this counted against him in the United States, increasing his menacing image in the eyes of some people within the dominant culture. Mr. King was a large man, and his size only escalated the presumed threat he posed. Over decades, people in the United States have accepted and assimilated the stereotype of African American men as criminals who are violent and dangerous. Often, whites cross the street when confronted with the sight of an African American man walking toward them. My students talked about such occurrences with incredulity and anger. "What are they afraid of?" they'd ask. Although these students were altruistic individuals who, over the years, had helped a wide variety of people, they were shunned because of a combination of the color of their skin, their social class, and their gender. Rodney King stood accused then of being black, large, and male, a frightening combination to some people, who translated his physical attributes into assumptions that he was violent, unpredictable, and threatening. As one juror commented, "He was obviously a dangerous person, massive size and threatening actions . . . Mr. King was controlling the whole show."[1]

One of the officers at the trial spoke of how they kept hitting Mr. King because he would not stay down. An African American man who will not stay down, in both a literal and figurative sense, is viewed by some as intolerable. The jury ruled that the force used against Mr. King was justifiable. The message implicit in this verdict was that people in the dominant white culture were justified in doing whatever they needed to do to keep African Americans and other people of color in their place. The implied racism in this message, which came through with great clarity to residents of South-Central Los Angeles and many others, served to intensify the latent rage in the hearts of those living in South-Central Los Angeles, those who have suffered abuse themselves at the hands of the police acting as agents of control and intimidation for the society at large.

By 5:30 P.M. on the afternoon the verdict was announced, violence had erupted at the corner of Florence and Normandie Avenues in South-Central Los Angeles. Law enforcement officials were conspicuous by their absence as an angry group dragged a number of motorists from their vehicles, beat them, hurled rocks and bottles, and looted a nearby liquor store. A television crew hovered overhead in a helicopter and transmitted the images of violence to living rooms across the city, further inflaming people.

When the burning and looting finally ended, over fifty people had been killed, and the property damage was well over $700 million. Los Angeles had been effectively shut down for the duration of the unrest. Unlike the unrest in 1965, this uprising was not confined to the Watts community. In 1992, areas affected by the unrest included many neighborhoods in Los Angeles city proper as well as a wide array of communities, including the San Fernando Valley, Pasadena, El Monte, Rowland Heights, Pomona, Hollywood, Beverly Hills, West Hollywood, Culver City, Compton, Harbor City, San Pedro, and Long Beach.[2] The community of Watts was also affected during this latest unrest, but, as one resident of the Nickerson Gardens government housing project in Watts stated, "We didn't have too much left anyway. We as black people in this community have nothing to protect."[3] The looting and burning spread across Los Angeles into communities that were thought to be relatively safe havens from the crime, violence, and resulting fear that affected South-Central Los Angeles. What started in some cases as peaceful protests broke into violence as people became more enraged by the verdict and the messages implicit in it. The unrest in 1992, compared to that in 1965, resulted in almost twice as many deaths, more than twice as many injuries, over four times as many arrests, and over four times as much property damage.[4] It was the worst case of civil unrest in the United States in this century, and when it was over, life for residents of the communities in South-Central Los Angeles did not fall back into the old patterns. Such ordinary daily tasks as shopping for food or doing laundry suddenly were fraught with difficulty because many establishments had been burned to the ground.

The shortage of supermarkets with competitive prices in the area was a problem before the civil unrest. People who have no means of transportation tend to shop close to home, and in Watts and other South-Central Los Angeles communities, this often meant the small, higher-priced corner grocery stores, many of which were owned by recent immigrants from, for example, South Korea. Tensions between African Americans and Korean Americans mirrored that which I observed between my African American and Latino students in that their relationship was marked by a lack of intercultural competence and experience, a lack of knowledge, and possession of distorted and inaccurate information about the other group. Some of the students I knew at Medgar High spoke of Korean American shopkeepers in their neighborhood with a clear lack of either respect or understanding; indeed, some students did not know they were of Korean origin and referred to them as Chinese. They expressed irritation that some of the shopkeepers seemed suspicious when the students walked into their stores and that they spoke so little English.

Victor related that he asked one Korean American shopkeeper if he could use his telephone to call his father because he was being confronted by gang members who were waiting for him outside the store. Victor was angry that the man "acted like he didn't understand English." In Victor's perception, the man was pretending not to understand so as to not allow him to use the telephone. Victor said, "This guy knows me. I go in there and buy stuff all the time." He responded to the shopkeeper with disrespect. Some of the African American patrons of stores owned by Korean Americans maintained that the store owners with whom they interacted treated them with a marked lack of respect; some of the store owners had the same complaint about their African American customers. Korean Americans may have been operating under the effects of the negative images and stereotypes of African

Americans, especially African American males, portrayed by the media in the United States. These media images were generally their only knowledge of African Americans, resulting in their suspiciousness and resultant behavior toward them.

Many African Americans also lacked intercultural competence and had few constructive opportunities to interact with the Korean Americans as real people rather than as stereotypes. Some felt anger that once again, as in the days leading up to the civil unrest in 1965, businesses within their community were owned by people who did not live there. They were further angered by the impression that the Korean Americans had been able to start new small business in the form of grocery stores, laundries, and liquor stores while this opportunity had been often denied to them through red-lining by banks and other financial institutions, the lack of assistance to prospective African American entrepreneurs to start small businesses, and institutional discrimination. Because African Americans often did not understand the culture of the other group, they did not know that many Koreans had brought money with them when they came to this country so that they had the capital necessary to start a new venture when they arrived. Further, the Koreans' sense of ethnic solidarity helped them to gather capital through the initiation of a *kae*, a credit-rotating system in which a group of Koreans pooled their resources and then made a loan to a group member who paid it back with interest, at which point the next group member was given a loan.[5] Finally, a customary Korean American business practice is for the entire family to contribute many hours of work within the family business. Such practices helped the businesses succeed but also curtailed job opportunities for nonfamily—that is, community—members.

Thus, members of both groups lacked understanding and intercultural competence. This lack was exacerbated by the language barrier, which lead to misunderstandings, hostility, and suspicion. Tensions between the African Americans and recent Korean immigrants intensified in 1991 when Soon Ja Du, a Korean American grocery store owner, shot and killed a young African American girl named Latasha Harlins after they argued over whether the girl had been attempting to steal a bottle of juice. As the girl walked away, Soon Ja Du shot her in the back of the head.[6] She was sentenced to five years of probation for the girl's death.

Because of the boiling resentment that grew out of this tragedy over what many people in the community felt was the terribly light penalty that resulted, Korean American merchants were especially hard hit by the looting and burning when the civil unrest of 1992 began. It was not easy to find a grocery store left standing in many neighborhoods in South-Central Los Angeles, and those still standing were empty, their contents removed by the looters. Those people who had a means of transportation reported that they had to drive well outside their communities to get such basic items as food and staples or to do their laundry. Certainly, life became more difficult for the residents after the civil unrest. Some residents, however, expressed the hope that in five years everything would be rebuilt and beautiful. Those who hold a historical perspective and may be, as a consequence, more realistic wonder upon what foundation such hopes are built: a look at Detroit or Washington, D.C., or even Watts reveals damage done in the uprisings in the 1960s which to this day has not been repaired. As Johnnie Tillman-Blackston, a retired laundry worker and city employee who lives in Watts commented, "I wonder if things will be different now than they were after Watts [the 1965 civil unrest]. The folks who saw the change after Watts were the ones who didn't live here, who came, got the money, and went back to their own neighborhoods after 5 o'clock in the evening."[7]

After the 1992 civil unrest, some people condemned attempts to explain it, maintaining that those who offered explanations of causal factors were apologists for the so-called rioters. The view that the uprising was begun by a violent few and furthered by compliant mobs who were greedy and wanted to procure something for nothing is arguably simplistic. People looted for a variety of reasons. The verdict touched a point of latent rage over the societal inequities in the United States, and the rage spilled out into the streets in violence and burning. For some, the looting was a statement that society has offered so little to them that it was now their turn to get something back. "We've been mad for so many years, and people have been trying to let frustration out," said one unemployed warehouseman who participated in the looting.[8] They felt they deserved what they took. For others, it was simply a chance to join in and procure items they would not be able to afford otherwise. Some people saw the looting on the television, realized the police were failing to respond, and joined in by going out on the streets to loot themselves. Need was a strong motive for some of those involved. One seventeen-year-old Latino who took three beds said, "I got bunk beds for my little brother and sister, and a bed for myself because I sleep on the floor."[9]

The account of the civil unrest in Watts in 1965 as described in the Kerner Commission Report[10] corresponds eerily to the occurrences in South-Central Los Angeles in 1992, twenty-seven years later. Indeed, descriptions of civil disorder in the 1960s in cities such as Chicago, Cleveland, Houston, Tampa, Washington, D.C., Cincinnati, Atlanta, Newark, and Detroit, to name a few, correspond with compelling accuracy to the descriptions of civil unrest in South-Central Los Angeles in 1992. Historians speak of the importance of studying history, of remembering the past in order to avoid repeating the same mistakes. However, in the case of urban unrest, it appears that those in positions of political and economic power in the United States have been oblivious to both our history and its looming and inevitable repetition.

The unrest in the cities in the 1960s was caused by a variety of factors, including confrontations with police and police brutality, strained and hostile community-police relations, inequity of social and economic justice between the "haves" and "have-nots," economic and educational inequalities, lack of medical care and medical insurance, joblessness, lack of community resident-owned businesses, lack of recreational and job training programs for youth, and racial tension. This reads like a description of causal factors for the civil unrest in 1992 in South-Central Los Angeles. Conditions in these communities have not changed for the better; they have, in many ways, only become worse.

The absurdly inaccurate rhetoric of then-President George Bush blaming the social programs of the 1960s for the civil uprising of 1992 was an irresponsible distortion of existing facts. These programs did help to lift people out of poverty, to feed pregnant women and children, to provide early educational experiences for children, and to protect the well being of the elderly. Their shortcoming was that they did not reach all those in need for long enough to bring about permanent positive changes in living conditions and life chances. Funding was, in large measure, transferred from the "War on Poverty," the programs of the Johnson administration, to the war in Vietnam, and, as funding was withdrawn, the seeds of unrest were replanted in the soil of discontent in Watts and other communities in South-Central Los Angeles.

Reductions in funding for these programs continued throughout the 1970s and 1980s, further crippling their effectiveness.

As business after business burned in South-Central Los Angeles in the last days of April 1992, some people outside the community commented that the violence was an absurd reaction to the verdict in the trial of the four LAPD officers. "They're burning down their own community!" they cried, shaking their heads in disbelief. However, these people lacked understanding on two points. The burning that resulted from the verdict was neither simply a self-destructive act nor solely a reaction to the verdict. The "King verdict," as it has become known, was the final straw for those who had watched the gap grow between the "haves" and the "have-nots" over the past fifteen years. Further, the people involved in the civil unrest were not, in a sense, burning their own community because far too few of them were able to have a stake in the community beyond merely living there. They owned few businesses. They were overcharged when they made purchases at the local "mom and pop" stores they often had to frequent because of the lack of major supermarkets in the neighborhoods or their lack of transportation to supermarkets elsewhere. They saw their money leave their hands and go into the coffers of people who drove away each day to their homes in other communities. The money of the residents was all too often drained out of the community in this fashion.

At the heart of the problem are the issues of ethnicity, race, and social class. It is inaccurate to simply say that the 1965 Watts civil unrest repeated itself twenty-seven years later. This description points out the similarities in social conditions but does not explore the worsening of those conditions and the differences between the two uprisings. In 1960, 80.6 percent of the population in Los Angeles County was white, 9.6 percent Latino, 7.6 percent African American, and 1.9 percent Asian and American Indian. By 1990, a dramatic shift had taken place; 40.8 percent of the residents of Los Angeles County were white, 37.8 percent Latino, 10.5 percent African American, and 10.5 percent Asian and American Indian.[11] Thus, the population of Los Angeles County underwent tremendous shifts in thirty years. The white population decreased by 50 percent, while the Latino population tripled. The African American population grew by 3 percent, and the Asian and American Indian population grew by 8.6 percent. Communities such as Watts experienced shifts in which the African American population began to be replaced as the majority by the rapidly increasing Latino population. As mentioned earlier, these two groups often have little knowledge of each other's culture, and the tension within the community resulting from this lack of mutual understanding was evident at Medgar High when we experienced conflicts between groups of African American and Latino students in the spring of 1990. With this demographic shift in the community caused by the increase in the Latino population, competition for scarce resources only exacerbated the already existing tension. Thus, the situation in Watts and other South-Central communities in 1992 was significantly worse, in many ways, than it was during the 1965 Watts civil unrest, considering the flight of industry; the decrease in blue-collar jobs caused, for example, by the closing of the Firestone, Lockheed, and GM plants; the lack of financial institutions and available investment capital; the destruction and suffering associated with drug usage; and the advent of rapidly increasing numbers of AIDS cases in the inner city.

Many of the problems encountered by people in Watts and other inner-city communities in the United States were caused by racism, classism, and ethnocentrism. The media focused their attention on the sensational and the negative, perpetuating a skewed vision of people of color who lived in the inner city. Students at Medgar High who saw the press arrive at the school wondered aloud what negative occurrence had brought them there and asked the media representatives why they never reported any of the positive accomplishments and occurrences at the school. Perhaps the explanation that was closest to the truth was that the news media printed what sold, and violence, crime, and sensationalism sold. Although I tried repeatedly to secure media coverage from mainstream sources for my students on the wide variety of altruistic activities in which they were involved, such coverage was not to be found. A gang killing in the neighborhood was of interest, but a group of inner-city kids making sack lunches for homeless people on Skid Row each week was not. Parents irate over the violence in the community was of interest, but eighteen students from Watts presenting a workshop on race relations at a state conference was not. The arrest of a young African American man accused of murder in a drive-by shooting was of interest; a young African American man being a mentor to a little boy, playing ball and talking with him to help him stay out of gangs and away from drugs, was not. The picture of South-Central Los Angeles and its residents that many people outside of these communities have formed is flawed, distorted, and incomplete. This kind of negative press has the effect of demonizing the poor, those of color, by broadcasting frightening images so that the stereotypes are only reinforced, never dispelled or debunked.

Father Gregory Boyle, pastor of Dolores Mission Church in East Los Angeles, said,

> I've buried twenty-six kids since I came to this parish. I always look back at Karen Toshima and the response that was immediate when she was killed on a street in Westwood [a wealthy predominantly white community in West Los Angeles]. Thirty special detectives, a foot patrol and a $35,000 reward were offered. I've never seen any of those things here and I've buried twenty-six kids who were killed in the same way. It's clear that one life in Westwood is worth twenty-six in Boyle Heights [a low-income minority community in East Los Angeles].[12]

As long as such inequities exist, the problems in communities like Watts will continue to grow unabated. As an eighteen-year-old Latino said, "Just because it's labeled as the ghetto doesn't mean it has to be."[13]

Political leaders and social planners in the United States need to listen to the voices of community members in Watts and other inner-city communities. The residents bear witness to the existing problems and understand the kinds of changes that need to be implemented. A dialogue needs to exist between the people of the community and those involved in the rebuilding effort. The appointment of Peter Ueberroth as the leading force in redevelopment efforts in the wake of the civil unrest missed the central issue: people become stakeholders in their own community by being actively involved in its creation or, in this case, recreation. Mr. Ueberroth, however well intentioned, was a wealthy white business executive and an outsider. People in the community were not consulted about his appointment. Leadership from within the community was not sought. The central point is that the redevelopment effort cannot be another "project" that comes from the outside in which other people decide what will be best for those within the community.

Considering the burdens they have had to bear, the anger of inner-city residents is both understandable and justified. When I taught at Medgar High, my students who were peer counselors did a skit to illustrate the importance of refraining from taking on everyone else's problems and burdens to the point of self-damage. A peer counselor walked across the room, and other students asked her to do them a favor and hold a book, a backpack, a bag, a coat, or a purse. The peer counselor accepted each new item until she was so overloaded that she began to stagger and finally fell to her knees when one last student foisted a bulging backpack onto her already considerable burden. Many of the residents of South-Central Los Angeles are like that student, finally overloaded and brought to their knees by the growing stressors of living in poverty, and many have responded in rage to the burdens an unresponsive society has handed to them. "Would you hold this? Just a little more poverty, a little more joblessness, a little more police brutality, a little more medically preventable illness . . . ?" The incredulity and lack of comprehension of some members of the dominant culture in response to the civil unrest in South-Central Los Angeles only illustrated how insulated people had become from the realities of the long-term poor, the working poor, and other disenfranchised people in the United States.

In the United States, our infant mortality rate rises and an increasing number of our children go hungry while we condemn the human rights abuses of other countries. We live in a society in which it is easier to procure a gun than it is to get health care or to register to vote. Mothers receiving AFDC to support their children are verbally attacked with the insinuation that they are lazy and want to receive something for nothing, yet the vast majority of the middle class looks passively at, for example, the government bailouts of the savings and loans and the Chrysler Corporation or federal government subsidies to agribusiness and oil and mining companies. White-collar crime, that is, "crime in the suites" as opposed to crime in the streets, is often overlooked or only mildly condemned; crime committed by the poor is a threat to the fabric of society, causing people to cry out for more prisons, more law enforcement, and more repressive laws to protect the wealth of the few against the needs of the many.

Toward the end of the civil unrest in South-Central Los Angeles, I was finally able to get through by telephone to some of my former students in Watts. I learned to my great relief that they had escaped physical harm, although they were in despair at the destruction within their community, the antisocial actions of others in the community, and the lack of such essentials as food, gasoline, public transportation, and electricity. Aracely, the strong, scrappy young women described earlier, said, "I'm ashamed of my people. I feel like all I worked for during four years [in the peer counseling program] is gone." Then her voice grew stronger as she told me she had been wearing her FIGHT RACISM T-shirt since the civil unrest began (a shirt all of the peer counselors wore to school and to conferences), saying that some people had stared at her and others had given her the "thumbs-up" sign. Aracely, Mari, Victor, and others continue to try to offer assistance, to educate, and to empower. Every phone call ended with the words "I love you." I see these vital young people as agents of hope rising from the ashes in South-Central Los Angeles.

The warning signs for the advent of civil unrest were clear and unmistakable. Indeed, the first five chapters of this book, written before the 1992 civil unrest, describe the causes behind the conditions of life in Watts, and these were the causal factors of the uprising. The 1992 civil unrest in South-Central Los Angeles that spread beyond its "red-lined" borders should be considered a wake-up call for the United States, our second and possibly final wake-up call. Now more than ever, we need to shift our focus from assigning blame to analyzing contributory causes and pushing for ameliorative action. Such an analysis and suggestions for change are the subject of the last chapter.

CHAPTER 7

Suggestions for Change

Several common threads run through many of the problems confronted by people in Watts and other inner-city communities: hope, power, opportunity, and equity. In most cases, it is the absence of these four essentials which contributes to the problems. Thus, the infusion of hope, power, opportunity, and equity into the community of Watts would help to engender positive social change.

The bulk of this chapter will be devoted to demonstrating the interrelated nature of and proposing solutions for each of the problem areas discussed in previous chapters and discussing the possible repercussions of continued inactivity.

FAMILY LIFE

The difficulties surrounding family life in Watts, such as child care, adolescent maternity, dysfunctional families, abuse, and generational blurring, are firmly intertwined. Many of the problems associated with family life in the inner city revolve around the central issue of adolescent maternity. Thus, this seems an appropriate place to begin.

Adolescent pregnancy is a contributor to the feminization of poverty in the United States. With more than a million adolescent pregnancies each year, the repercussions of early initiation of sexual activity are apparent. What can be done about adolescent pregnancy? We know that low birthweight and infant mortality are two of the many manifestations of adolescent pregnancy,[1] and that the children are at risk in utero. Intervention prior to pregnancy is needed, and such intervention can take the form of education in anatomy, male and female sexual functioning, the use of contraceptives, and communication with sexual partners and parents regarding sex. Education can continue in the form of values clarification and self-inquiry into adolescents' motivation regarding high-risk sexual behaviors to increase their self-awareness and self-knowledge. As pointed out in Chapter 2, many adolescents in Watts become involved in high-risk sexual behaviors because of exceedingly low self-esteem; becoming pregnant or impregnating another was viewed as one method of proving womanhood or manhood for adolescents burdened with poor self-esteem and possessing few realms in which they could succeed. Thus, programs geared toward increasing self-esteem, when presented in conjunction with other methods of educational intervention, may prove effective.

Any of the above methods can be taught in schools, and children need to be reached at an early age with clearly explained, explicit information on sexual functioning and intensive work in values clarification and self-esteem. Those who maintain that giving young people knowledge of sexual functioning will encourage them to become sexually active are misinformed. When people are asked to function in ignorance, it is probable that mistakes will occur, and in these cases, the mistakes involve tremendous tolls on human lives and high costs to society.

School-based clinics such as the one at Medgar High are helpful in maintaining the health of students of low-income families and in providing much-needed sexual information, physical examinations, and pregnancy and STD testing, as well as information on contraception and STD protection. Within the northern industrialized countries, the United States has the highest rate of adolescent pregnancy,[2] yet funding for family-planning clinics has been rapidly decreasing throughout the 1980s and early 1990s. When family-planning information is not available at school or at a school-based clinic, then community-based family-planning clinics may be the places of last resort for those adolescents who are motivated enough to seek needed information. Funding for school-based clinics and for family-planning clinics, both of which serve a tremendous need, especially for low-income women, must be allocated at the state, federal, and local or community levels.

Finally, the community itself, in this case the community of Watts, needs to begin to foster a shift in values by creating a positive value for delaying sexual intercourse, using "safer sex" methods including contraception, and deferring childbearing until the prospective parents are economically self-sufficient and stable. As long as early childbearing has an associated positive or even neutral value within the community, it will continue to thrive as one method by which young people within the community can receive recognition, praise, and approval.

After all intervention methods have failed in preventing a pregnancy, family planning services which are readily available would help young women determine if they are pregnant. These young women in Watts are at increased risk of maternal mortality and pregnancy complications, and their babies are at risk for infant mortality, low birthweight, and chronic disabling conditions. The solution is clearly feasible and inexpensive: prenatal care. Prenatal care is estimated to cost between $500 and $1,000, as opposed to the $250,000 lifelong price tag associated with medical care for a low-birthweight infant.[3] Indeed, some evidence shows that women who are offered high-quality sliding-fee prenatal health care in which they pay what they can afford may be more likely to stay out of the social welfare system, learn to manage their financial resources, and begin to be involved in decision making related to childbearing in terms of the expenses they themselves can bear, which is the first step in responsible family planning.[4]

In conjunction with prenatal care, adolescent mothers need other special assistance. Medicaid and the Special Supplemental Feeding Program for Women, Infants, and Children (WIC) involve tremendous amounts of paperwork and a long application process. Both could be simplified to extend their outreach. Many women in Watts do not have private medical insurance and are ineligible for Medicaid, which means they are without prenatal care of any kind. This was often the case for young women I knew in Watts who saw a doctor for the first time during their pregnancy when they delivered their babies in the emergency rooms of the county hospital. Medicaid benefits could be extended to cover this segment of the population.

Outreach to these women may encourage them to receive prenatal care. Women within the community could be trained as resource people or mentors who would then visit prospective mothers and offer them nutrition information, transportation, and assistance with paperwork and with appointment reminders. They could initiate parenting classes to help educate new parents about child and adolescent development, parenting skills, effective and nonviolent strategies for coping with child discipline problems, and nonabusive methods of enforcing rules. These community mentors could be involved in outreach to substance abusers who become pregnant to help them stay drug-free during their pregnancies. Such community-based options empower individuals in inner-city communities like Watts, creating solidarity and a sense of civic pride while expanding job opportunities.

Finally, once these children are born, they are at risk for disease and malnutrition. In 1982, the school lunch program, which often is the one nutritious meal inner-city children eat each day, was modified so that a million children were made ineligible.[5] Children who are hungry do not learn. Funding for school lunch programs, immunizations, and increased medical care is cost-effective in the same way prenatal care is cost-effective. A relatively small early investment may preclude the need for later expensive intervention.

ACADEMIC SUCCESS AND FAILURE

With regard to academic performance, the argument is similar: society can invest early or pay dearly later. Education is the foundation of the changes needed to improve the life chances of all members of society in the United States. If the education that people in South-Central Los Angeles are receiving is of poor quality, they will lack the requisite skills to compete in a highly competitive labor market. Our first priority needs to be greatly increased state and federal funding for high-quality kindergarten through twelfth-grade education. The current budget cuts in California, for example, have severely disabled the education programs offered in the state. Education needs to be a top priority item in state and federal budgets. We need to reverse the current trend as education continues to drop in the state and federal governments' priority ranking scheme.

This is not to say that education should move toward a voucher system, which some people are advocating. Voucher systems would to a large degree destroy public education and create an even greater disparity in educational equity than we are currently experiencing. Under the voucher system, schools would be able to choose their students. In short, students with special needs or behavioral problems, exceptional children, children living in poverty who have had poor early educational experiences, and limited and non-English speakers, to name a few, could be excluded. These are the students who require more rather than less educational intervention, which translates into more education dollars. Thus, under a voucher system, those who need the most would receive the least. *Equitable* does not mean *equal* in education. It means we must offer education to each child according to his or her needs, which by definition means that some children will require more than others to achieve similar outcomes or to function up to their potential. Those students most at risk for this inequitable education are inner-city students of color who often have had a poor education from the start, are often in need of remediation because of the poor quality of the education offered to them, and are among the most demonized and maligned of our nation's youth precisely because they are children of color living in the inner city. Under a voucher system, they will be warehoused in schools of last resort, even more effectively denied access to equitable educational opportunities. Thus, through the voucher system, the race and class divisions in Los Angeles schools are likely to become more pronounced. The focus must be on creating a fully funded, equitable public education system so as to provide *all* children with a quality education.

In addition to adequate and equitable state and federal funding, private business could become involved with school districts in helping to create job training programs geared toward the needs of participating businesses with the understanding that hiring for available positions would be from the pool of individuals participating in the job training courses. This is not to say that public education should be privatized. However, the private sector benefits from the public education system; it is time for those who benefit to give back to their communities.

Children who live in poor families lack the resources of their middle-class and wealthy counterparts. Those who have the financial resources are able to secure access to educational day care; private kindergarten; private elementary and secondary education; private tutoring; and private instruction in such areas as music, dance, art, computers, and theater. Children who live in poverty are not able to access such resources. Since, they do not receive the enriched early educational experiences of their more advantaged agemates, they arrive at the schoolhouse door without the early introduction to concepts that leads to a smooth transition into school. Such inequities damage the nation just as clearly as they hurt the poor. Being encumbered with a large uneducated population living in poverty is a sure road to economic and social disaster for the United States. Refraining from taking strong measures to ensure that quality education is available for everyone is akin to refusing to bail out a sinking boat because you do not like some of the other passengers. For your own survival, you may need to set aside private prejudices and strive for the common good. If not, everyone drowns. Thus, it seems clear that children of all socio-economic backgrounds need a rigorous education, one which involves their parents and guardians in the educational process.

Intensive early education programs work, programs which begin with very small children and which are geared toward teaching and discovery learning, not custodial care. Chronic poverty can lead to intergenerational dysfunction and cause developmental problems, including intellectual dysfunction, which can be remedied by intensive early education.[6] These early educational experiences are strongly tied to later academic performance and achievement. Since children in poverty are by definition at risk for developmental delays, this intensive early intervention may be the one factor which will help them begin to achieve to their potential.

Early childhood education programs for children living in poverty such as Head Start are already in existence, and these programs could be the foundation for early intervention. The programs would require some modifications, particularly in the area of academics, but the changes would be relatively minor and would entail little extra cost. Many children who could benefit are not being reached by these programs, and community outreach groups could help to identify those children and place them in an appropriate program in their neighborhood.

Perhaps the best solutions for the public education system in Los Angeles will be those which suggest radical measures for restructuring the huge district. The following suggestions could function as part of that restructuring. Management of neighborhood schools needs to be placed in the hands of school-based councils composed of teachers, students, administrators, parents, community leaders, and nonteaching staff. Such a decision-making body would reduce the need for the currently existing number of administrators in districts that are administratively top-heavy. Upward mobility for teachers in Los Angeles Unified School District, as in many other districts, is confined to entering administration. Quality teaching is not rewarded in the existing system; the pay increases the further a teacher moves away from the classroom into the administrative ranks. Administrators' pay can be double, triple, or even quadruple that of the classroom teacher.

For example, Medgar High School, commonly thought of as the least desirable school at which to teach in the district, was called the "Administrative Academy" by some teachers at the school. Their contention was that the school was overloaded with administrators and that the district sent administrators to Medgar High for training under the assumption that their experience at Medgar High would prepare them to work in administration at any school within the district. Such a revolving door policy toward administration in the 1980s created a tangible lack of stability. Because Medgar High is not considered by many people to be a choice assignment in the district, an attitude of indifference often predominated. One administrator who was under fire for the condition of her department sighed and said to me, "So what's the worst thing they could do to me? Send me to Medgar High? I'm already here."

Those individuals who are truly drawn to administration, who have an administrative credential, and who are approved by the school site council as previously described would be placed in South-Central Los Angeles schools. They would work with the school site council in order to supervise the operation of the school. The council would rule on all matters pertaining to the operation of the school, including budgetary allocations. The administrator at the school would have an equal voice with other council members and would be responsible for keeping the group informed about laws, regulations, and district policies outside the knowledge base of the group as well as for instituting the policy decisions of the council. All administrators and ex-administrators would no longer be paid according to the inflated administrative salary schedule when they leave their positions or are reassigned but would return to the teaching salary schedule. Just as classroom teachers who take on special assignments are sometimes given a stipend for those extra duties, so would the administrators be given a stipend for the extra responsibilities of their positions. All administrators would be required to teach at least one-entry level course within their original discipline each year so that they would maintain awareness of classroom realities, including the needs of the teachers and the student population. Those administrators currently in South-Central Los Angeles schools who are not accepted in the limited slots would return to the classroom, to be paid at the same rate as classroom teachers.

The priorities within the Los Angeles Unified School District seem skewed away from education toward support services, and this is the case in many public education districts across the country. Thus, some support staff are better paid than classroom teachers, and the salaries of all district employees may be tied to those of classroom teachers, which means that if teachers receive a raise, all other district employees receive a raise at the same rate. Los Angeles Unified School District teachers who went out on strike in 1989 were aghast when told by some administrators that they were demonstrating stupidity by going on strike and losing pay for each day they were out; the administrators were at school, lost no pay, and still received the same increase. Then-president of United Teachers Los Angeles Wayne Johnson in a 1989 edition of his column in *United Teacher* described how, if striking teachers received a 10 percent pay raise, the other 78,000 district employees, including administrators, would receive the same raise. He said, "A 10 percent raise will give a $23,000 beginning teacher . . . a $2,300 increase, up to a whopping $25,300 . . . That same 10 percent will get Leonard Britton [then the Los Angeles Unified School District superintendent] a $14,000 raise to $155,000. His chauffeur will get a $9,000 raise to $99,000 . . . A school police officer will get a $4,800 raise to $52,800. And a beginning locksmith with a high school education and six months training will get a $3,500 raise to $39,385."[7] Teachers in the classrooms are told they must take more students into their already overcrowded classrooms, do without books for their students, and battle for supplies. These measures are difficult to adjust to when one sees the superintendent with a chauffeur who makes four times the salary of a beginning teacher. It becomes obvious in analyzing the remuneration assigned to these different positions that the priority in this district is not teachers, students, and the process of educating; it is perpetuating an entrenched bureaucracy. This perspective needs to change if the district is ever to become a viable purveyor of quality education.

Just the act of doing away with the bloated administrative salary schedule would release large sources of funding which could then be profitably used at the school sites. As a result, several teachers could be hired for each ex-administrator, which would result in decreased class sizes and better education. Other administrative functions could be turned over to interested classroom teachers who would rotate into the positions on, for example, a two-year basis. Community members could be hired at an entry level to assist with these tasks, thus providing more job opportunities in the community and creating a school which could function as an important hub within the community.

Rather than allowing the continuation of de facto segregated schools, school clusters could be established in which several schools are combined at a central location. This differs from a program of busing minority children to predominantly white middle-class neighborhoods. Rather, its focus would be to create a quality schooling center which would draw from the student populations of several schools, creating an integrated educational community. This would create an ethnically diverse environment and help to foster the kinds of ethnic and racial understanding and cooperation that are so lacking and are in large measure contributors to the current conditions of racial tension and unrest in the United States.

Students who are educated with others of differing ethnicities, races, and cultures in an environment in which an appreciation of cultural diversity is encouraged and allowed to flourish are provided with an opportunity to see one another as familiar equals and potential allies rather than incomprehensible "others." Some of my students in Watts had never ventured beyond their immediate neighborhood in the inner city. Living fewer than fifteen miles from the Pacific Ocean, some had never seen it. Some had never had a chance to interact with a white peer until we began traveling to peer counseling conferences across the state of California. Their lives were so encapsulated that they did not have any knowledge of other cultures beyond those represented in the community and whatever stereotypical information they had acquired from movies and the media. One of my African American students came up to me at a conference with a young white student in tow. My student told me with much amazement, "This guy doesn't like to surf!" under the assumption that all white teenagers liked to surf. His new friend was equally amazed that my student didn't like to play basketball. These are, perhaps, small victories in the debunking of myths and resultant stereotypes that are based upon inaccurate or incomplete information about others. However, the joy of education lies in its exponential or ripple effect: each person teaches another.

As culturally diverse as the United States is, some of us have not yet realized that our potential strength lies not only in our diversity but also in our knowledge of one another and our appreciation of our differences and similarities. Schooling children together in cluster schools would be one step toward eliminating racism, classism, ethnocentrism, and xenophobia, which are based in large measure upon lack of knowledge and contact with others.

Effective teaching and quality teachers are inextricably tied together. Inner-city schools like Medgar High in Watts cannot attain a high level of excellence if they do not have the best possible staff. As long as inner-city schools are considered the "dumping ground" for poor or inexperienced teachers, the quality of educational output will remain poor. Even a few poor teachers at an inner-city school can have a profoundly negative effect in the education of alienated inner-city youth.[8]

A strong professional staff which is there by choice, drawn by attractive professional opportunities as well as by altruism, will help to reduce the tremendous turnover at inner-city schools, thus creating some sorely needed stability for the students. Districts and teacher preparation programs need to offer specialized training for those individuals interested in teaching in the inner city. Teachers in inner-city schools must be able to approach their students with respect and genuine affection. A strong background in multicultural education is a minimum prerequisite so that all educational activities are meaningful and relevant to the inner-city students. Teachers who are deemed sufficiently qualified to be offered an inner-city assignment should be appropriately compensated.

At all levels of education, institutional racism continues to exist in the United States. At times, it can be subtle; teachers and professors may do nothing overt, but they nonetheless may convey their personal biases with regard to such issues as ethnicity, race, class, and gender. At other times, it can be blatant, as shown by the lack of a multicultural, pluralistic perspective across the curriculum and in the textbooks. In either case, students internalize these messages, learning something about how powerful segments of society view them and how they, according to the dominant culture, should view themselves. Thus, teachers need to examine their own prejudices, and they need to be trained to teach in an equitable fashion using nonbiased materials. Class sizes should be reduced and should reflect a multicultural focus, that is, one which avoids a purely Eurocentric bias within the curriculum.

Inequities sweep beyond preschool through the twelfth grade into the realm of the university as well. College and university opportunities are often denied to those who are living in poverty. Effective Affirmative Action programs addressing the issue of socioeconomic status as well as minority status need to be implemented. These programs are still essential in creating a university community that reflects the population of the country. The poor are usually the first to be denied access to higher education. One of the main reasons given by my students who were accepted to a college or university for not attending or for leaving without completing their undergraduate studies was lack of funds. With the budget deficit in the state of California, for example, tuition at state universities is rising, and those most affected by such hikes in tuition fees are the poor. Many low-income students across the state are being forced to leave the university, not because they are incapable of completing their coursework but because they do not have the financial resources to pay the increasing tuition.

Programs such as Upward Bound which give low-income and minority students early experience on a college campus are extremely successful and need to be expanded to reach all interested students rather than the small percentage they are now able to reach. The problem in education is not that we do not know what to do or what will ameliorate the situation. We do. However, we seem to lack a societal commitment, the necessary funding, and trained personnel to implement those programs we know that work in order to reach all possible clients with the best possible educational experiences.

Adequate college counseling for high school students which includes assistance with financial aid would be helpful. Establishing a mentoring program at the college level in which a trained and informed faculty member is paired with an inner-city student would help students bridge the gap between the social environment in which they were raised and the new reality of the college campus. Further, peer counseling and tutoring programs can assist students at both the high school and college levels. Adolescents naturally turn to their peers for assistance with problems; well-trained tutors and youth counselors can provide much-needed academic assistance combined with personal understanding of students' life situations. Early and vigorous recruitment of minority youth into the teaching profession would create more classroom role models for inner-city students and would increase the pool of individuals of color who enter graduate school to attain master's and doctoral degrees. If inner-city public schools were fulfilling their mandate, quality education would be expected, and the specific recruitment of minority students for college and university would become unnecessary.

Scholarships and tuition waivers can be powerful incentives for prospective inner-city teachers and for inner-city students. As more people of color receive graduate degrees, they will then be available for employment at colleges and universities across the country, and will be in a strategic position to function as mentors and role models to incoming minority students, to debunk myths, and to dispel stereotypes and racist attitudes held by some individuals in the dominant culture.

The paucity of apprenticeship or vocational training programs for students who are not college bound limits students' post–high school options to those few available jobs that require minimal training and education. So much human potential is simply wasted. An apprenticeship program for noncollege-bound students would provide them with the incentive to remain in school and to acquire skills which would help them to secure employment and earn a living wage. Job training programs could be offered at public schools, utilizing the school site for as many hours a week as possible. At present, many schools are tremendously underutilized. Schools which are more responsive to the needs of the people within the communities they serve are more likely to be utilized to their fullest extent.

Schools are in an excellent position to coordinate community programs for early childhood education, parenting, nutrition, literacy, job training, substance abuse prevention, and mediation of community problems. However, these programs require adequate funding and a staff of qualified individuals with the appropriate expertise in these areas of need.

Once there is increased community involvement within the schools, greater focus could then be given to a literacy campaign, which is essential to changing the life options for people in South-Central Los Angeles. Individuals who cannot read cannot vote, and thus they are without a political voice in what occurs in their local community or in their country. Further, with functional and marginal illiteracy in the United States topping 60 million adults,[9] literacy becomes a target issue in children's academic achievement. The toll goes far beyond the painful personal experiences of an individual who cannot read and who becomes marginalized as a result of this inability.

Parents who read aloud to their children starting when the children are small prepare them to begin to read and offer powerful messages about the importance of reading for pleasure and information. Parents who read in the home further strengthen these messages to their children, making it more likely that the children will read. Thus, children of parents who are illiterate begin school with some clear disadvantages. A school-based literacy project in which parents and children can learn to read together would be an effective first step. While the children are in school, parents would be able to attend classes themselves, learning how to read. The classes could be an effective forum for offering educational opportunities in parenting skills and for providing parents with information on such topics as birth control, health care, nonviolent disciplinary techniques, and job training opportunities. Children would see their parents involved in learning and would be able to assimilate the message that learning is a positive activity. This form of intervention could help to establish a powerful alliance between school and home life. Classes could be made available during the regular school day, in the evenings, and on weekends to accommodate everyone, including working parents.

Many of these solutions will require additional funding. However, as with adolescent pregnancy, investments made now on proactive or prevention programs will represent a significant savings in the future. The United States needs the infusion of bright young minds to tackle the problems facing it in the coming decades, minds created through strong education and intellectual challenges. The future of the country lies within its ability to realize that equitable, quality education for all of its citizens who are interested in participating is not a luxury but a necessity. The country will find it increasingly difficult to compete in the world market unless it makes education an established, long-term priority in order to create the highly trained work force needed now and into the next century. Thus, it is in the interests of the United States to correct inequities in school funding and to provide an excellent education for all children, who in many ways represent the wealth of the nation.

GANGS

All of these social issues under discussion are linked to one another. Young people who defer childbearing until they are involved in a stable and financially secure relationship give birth to healthier babies whom they are less likely to abuse. These children, if given proper nutrition, attention, and education, are more likely to grow up with high aspirations, feeling secure within themselves and their families and more able to resist the recruiting activities of a gang.

Some individuals join gangs for economic reasons as described in Chapter 3. Young men in the inner city suffer from unemployment rates as high as 70 percent because of the disinvestment and deindustrialization in these areas. The sale of illicit drugs and weapons can help provide housing, pay for food for the family, or purchase those luxury items which may give them added prestige with their peers. For those who join gangs from a desire for material gains, more viable legitimate income alternatives may help to keep them involved in legal activities. Job training and legitimate employment opportunities offering a living wage are desperately needed.

Also needed is education in the form of violence prevention programs such as the one at Medgar High in Watts, and they need to start with very young children. Parents and teachers can be educated about the signs of gang involvement and effective methods of communicating with youth who are at risk for such activities. Peer counseling programs can be effective as part of the educational intervention, especially those which teach conflict management skills as alternatives to violence. Rites of passage based on ethnic traditions, for example, can be developed within the school or community framework so that adolescents have a sense of their approaching adulthood and involvement in the community.

Such nationwide actions as enacting more comprehensive and effective gun control laws may help to remove guns from the streets. Further, we need community-based police forces which reflect the population they serve and which are sensitive to its needs. This force could begin walking foot patrols in the inner city so that the officers are known to the residents and have a visible presence rather than simply being an alien force that arrives, often tardy, when trouble starts. Having a community-based police force may help to control acts of violence and illegal activities and may increase the sense of security within the neighborhood, creating a more cordial relationship between the community and the police.

Finally, full employment of minority youth and greatly improved educational opportunities in Watts and other inner-city communities would help to create a climate of hope. Again, such an investment in all of our young people is an investment in the future of the nation.

SUBSTANCE ABUSE

The community resource people who work with pregnant women and teach parenting classes could also be instrumental in identifying young people who are at risk for substance abuse. This could, in effect, help in the identification of preadolescents before they become involved with substance abuse, which in turn would reduce the number of lost school and work days, reduce the costs of medical care, and even reduce the loss of human life.

Since tobacco use represents a substantial health risk, intensive education programs at all grade levels on the dangers of its usage would be warranted. Beyond such educational intervention, a schoolwide ban on smoking may provide the message that the campus is drug-free.

Students need help with these issues because of the large amount of peer pressure involved with drug usage and possible abuse. Values clarification programs aimed at clarifying individuals' values, thoughts, and perceptions about all types of drug use may help students understand their own views. This kind of self-understanding helps young people begin to articulate their feelings and decisions about the use of alcohol and other drugs, which is important in learning how to resist peer pressure. Assertiveness training programs can be extremely effective in helping students learn how to respond assertively to peer pressure, and they were used with some success in the peer counseling programs I taught at Medgar High. In addition, conflict management training can be helpful in teaching students how to deal nonviolently with a conflict once it has occurred. Students are taught how to work toward an efficacious resolution to prevent the conflict from escalating into a violent episode.

Substance abuse often causes fetal damage that can result in low birthweight, birth defects, and stillbirths when women take drugs while they are pregnant. Educational intervention can greatly help in this area also. Practical information given to young people at an early age which conveys the dangers of alcohol and other drugs to the unborn may indeed help to keep some from using alcohol and other drugs while pregnant.

For those individuals who are coping with an addiction problem, drug treatment programs which are geared toward inner-city youth are vitally important. Just as reflective teachers modify their delivery from one class to the next, so drug treatment programs should be geared toward each particular audience. Inner-city youth will not necessarily buy into a program geared for members of the dominant culture. Treatment programs need to go beyond the simplistic "just say no" approach advocated in some prevention circles during the 1980s and early 1990s. This approach blames the victims of substance abuse if they find they are not strong enough to "just" say no; although it may sound easy, it can be agonizingly difficult. Such a simplistic approach ignores, for example, the factor of environmentally induced despair that often is the cause of drug abuse. Treatment upon demand is essential; we in this society cannot realistically ask people to "say no" to drugs without offering practical assistance to help effect such a difficult change.

Finally, the international narcotics industry must be seriously confronted to end the shipments of drugs into the United States. Powerful international drug cartels are collecting billions of dollars by capitalizing on the addictions of people like Carla, whom I described in the chapter on substance abuse. A solution to the substance abuse problem in the United States needs to be two-pronged, aimed at stopping both the imported supply and the internal social ills that produce the demand.

STRESS AND PREMATURE MORTALITY

Homicide claims far too many lives in the inner city. However, it is not the only cause of premature mortality in communities like Watts. Neoplasms and cardiovascular disease are leading causes of premature mortality among African American men. Serious support for research is needed to identify the leading causes of death in high mortality areas of the country such as Watts, and health care programs need to be implemented which include preventive medicine, early disease detection and diagnosis, and adequate medical treatment. School-based clinics are one way to begin to bring medical treatment and health education directly to young people and to help compensate for the lack of medical doctors within the community.

The stressors of life in poverty begin in utero. Until conditions can be changed in the inner city, stress management programs can be a useful part of all school curricula. Such programs could be adapted effectively for use with elementary school children, who would benefit emotionally and physically from being empowered at an early age with such skills.

Community resource groups, including those established in churches, could help to educate community members about the physical manifestations of stress, the resultant physical dangers, early detection of the warning signs of stress-induced illness, and stress management techniques. Such training could also take place within parenting classes so that the information could then be passed on to children as part of parenting skills. Finally, peer counselors within the school system could encourage dialogue with youth who are at risk, helping them to talk about their lives and teaching them stress management techniques.

Programs which encourage peer support, like the peer counseling program and the future teacher program I developed at Medgar High, can help to reduce the stress levels of inner-city youth by providing them with activities, outlets, and peer interactions which are positive and life-enhancing. Not all students fit into the programs currently offered at inner-city schools. Although educational sources encourage schools to offer after-school programs as an alternative to, for example, gang activities, the activities frequently are not varied enough to provide options for most students. If the focus is solely on athletics and the creative arts, a large percentage of students will not be served. Special-interest groups and clubs can offer a safe haven for many students, including, for example, those who are not doing well academically in school, those who are in some way considered and treated as social outcasts, and those who are shy. Once students are participating in such a program, they may find peer support and a forum in which they feel able to voice their feelings, two strong antidotes to the stressors of inner-city life. Programs which are varied and inclusive and which start in elementary school may help to channel students toward their interests and encourage cooperative group involvement. At inner-city schools like Medgar High, the list of electives is very short, reflecting the need of school personnel to focus on providing basic instruction and remediation at the expense of extracurricular activities. The graduation requirements demand that students' schedules have very little room for exploring the kinds of subjects historically presented in elective classes. However, these classes and their associated activities attract students and often provide them with a reason to stay in school. Thus, a varied curriculum that offers traditional educational opportunities and a strong program of electives and extracurricular activities may help to promote retention, especially for at-risk inner-city youth.

JOBLESSNESS

Once people have received education and/or job training, they need jobs which offer a living wage. In South-Central Los Angeles and the surrounding communities, 70,000 manufacturing jobs were lost between 1978 and 1982.[10] These were jobs that offered people a viable chance at supporting their families. The jobs that are available now pay less than minimum wage at textile sweatshops.[11]

Even when work is available in the community, it often does not go to community members. For example, in the Nickerson Gardens housing project, 85 percent of the residents are unemployed. When the Nickerson Gardens Day Care Center was built, which logically should have involved hiring residents, it was built by people from outside the community.[12] This is not unusual.

The residents of South-Central Los Angeles need meaningful employment. So many of the jobs have been exported to other countries where labor costs are extremely low. In their quest for increased capital accumulation, many U. S. companies are a key factor in causing the demise of the country's inner cities. Full employment needs dictate that manufacturers maintain their production facilities in the United States rather than exploit the labor forces in developing countries. The hemorrhage of jobs outside the country needs to be curtailed before the United States can hope to create a healthy economy which benefits a greatly increased percentage of its citizens and which could thereby offer hope to residents in the inner cities.

According to a report on minority youth employment released by the Los Angeles County Commission on Human Relations, minority youth are subjected to discriminatory practices in hiring and on the job. Further, transportation is a problem because many jobs are located outside the community, and guidance counselors are not giving appropriate and adequate guidance in terms of employment and career counseling.[13] Ameliorative measures for these problems could be fairly simple. A public youth employment agency which is centralized to bring together youth and potential training and job opportunities would be helpful. Few young people in Watts own and operate cars, and those who do often lack automobile insurance because of red-lining by insurance companies and the high cost of automobile insurance in inner-city communities. This condition makes it difficult for South-Central residents to commute to jobs outside the community. An expanded mass transit system which charged reasonably low fares would allow individuals to go to jobs further from their homes, a key to widening the potential job market for inner-city residents. Finally, the involvement of private industry could include early recruitment and training of inner-city adolescents and the use of van pools to transport people from their homes in the inner city to their job sites.

SERVICES

People in South-Central Los Angeles desperately need the financial services that one would expect to find in any community in the United States and that are inadequate or nonexistent in the community. Discriminatory bank policies and the scarcity of financial institutions, for example, are a part of the problem for the inner-city poor in this country. Because most banks have minimum deposit and/or minimum balance requirements, many people in Watts and other communities in South-Central Los Angeles are unable to open a bank account. Thus, they are unable to cash their checks at a bank and must rely on check-cashing services which provide the service for a percentage of the total amount. Consequently, people who are living in poverty have their income further reduced by having to pay for services that should be provided as a matter of course within their community. To address this problem, banks need to drop their minimum deposit and balance requirements, establish low-activity accounts for very small monthly fees, and actively recruit for accounts within the community.

The great irony of poverty is that the poor often end up paying more than the more affluent for such simple services as cashing a check, obtaining car insurance, or shopping for food. Those who are the least able to afford these extra costs are subjected to the added burden and resultant impediments and stressors. Food prices on many items in Watts are higher than the prices in, for example, predominantly white, middle-class West Hollywood. Car insurance rates are higher in Watts than in Beverly Hills, California. Individuals with high balances in their banking accounts receive financial services for no charge. These inequities are woven into the fabric of the society in the United States. Privilege and relative ease are accorded to the relatively well off or the affluent. Life is much more difficult for the poor even in common, everyday tasks, and many of these difficulties and much of the resultant stress could be easily remedied by the eradication of red-lining in housing and real estate, banking, and insurance.

SUMMARY

Adolescent out-of-wedlock maternity is a causal factor in the feminization of poverty. Adolescent, single parenthood increases the risk of child abuse, which can lead to decreased self-esteem and dysfunctional families. Low self-esteem and lack of a functional family structure contribute to the incidence of gang membership and substance abuse. All of these issues add to the high levels of stress involved in living in the inner city. Although each of the strands can be teased apart for closer examination, any viable solutions must involve the whole cloth rather than the separate threads. An attack on one problem in isolation will accomplish little. The problems must be attacked simultaneously on all fronts for lasting change to occur. As Michael Harrington pointed out, "If one problem is solved, and the others are left constant, there is little gain."[14]

A concerted effort to make changes in the inner city must mean by definition that the structures of United States society will have to change. A form of mini-apartheid exists in the United States which allows the continued existence of deteriorating inner cities, actual cities-within-cities, in which the majority of the residents are people of color and are among the long-term poor. The inherent racism and classism behind the psychology of "blaming the victim" needs to be eradicated. In addition, social programs such as those outlined in this chapter need to be initiated, creating a cycle of health rather than disease. The infusion into Watts of jobs, adequate and safe housing, medical care, quality education, and child care options could lead to increased opportunities for inner-city residents. Residents would experience an increase of communal pride and individual self-esteem which might well decrease gang membership, adolescent pregnancy, violent acts, and substance abuse. Such a decrease in these nonefficacious activities would undoubtedly create healthier communities, attracting the businesses and services which have left the inner city and whose departure helped to foster its decline. This infusion of business would in turn create more jobs, and the cycle would continue its spiral toward health and hope rather than decay and despair.

Such massive changes will take more than money; they also will take time. The United States did not reach its current state quickly. It took years to create the present two-tiered, discriminatory economic system and societal structure which have led to economic exploitation and a lack of opportunities, engendering the long-term poverty and eventual loss of hope seen in Watts and other inner cities. A legacy of discrimination and restricted economic opportunity that has been passed along for generations has caused the long-term poor to make a realistic and painfully accurate negative appraisal of their conditions and opportunities.

It will take time to eradicate the hopelessness in Watts and in other inner-city communities in the United States. It may take even longer to cultivate a value for a pluralistic society on a national level, and yet it is just such a society of vision for social justice that needs to be encouraged. Considering the powerfully destructive results of continuing of the status quo, we as a nation have much to gain by acting quickly and decisively.

EPILOGUE

Leaving my teaching position in Watts was much more difficult and painful than I had ever imagined. I had gone to teach at Medgar High out of a sense of social conscience; I wanted to move beyond just talking about issues of social justice to being actively involved in such issues in the area I knew best, that of education.

I had questions I wanted to answer about poverty, stereotypes, ethnicity/race and class relations, inner cities, and my own role as an individual in this society in perpetuating social injustice, at the very least by being ill-informed. The questions were, in great measure, answered, although the answers sparked new and more profoundly disturbing questions.

As I left I was vividly aware that my time teaching in Watts was voluntary; I could leave when I decided it was time to do so. Since that leave-taking, I have continued to ponder the simple and stark reality that many of the students I knew, people of such bright promise and fierce pride, did not have that same choice I had. They could not leave when they decided it was time to do so. Their options were limited by the issues I have tried to present in this book. The invisible yet palpable wall around the inner city contains them as surely as if it were composed of fences topped with concertina wire and guard towers.

For the rest of my life, I will remember the people I knew in Watts, their faces, their voices, their stories. I will retain the image of Colette sitting so straight, head held high as she spoke of the insufferable abuses in her life, filled with dignity as a single tear like a crystal drop made a path down her lovely cheek. This is the image of Watts for me, my metaphor for Watts: the dignity in the face of great suffering and pain.

I promised my students I would write about their lives, to use the written word to help people see beyond the negative stereotypes and media portrayals. I have tried to be faithful to that promise.

NOTES

INTRODUCTION

1. Ann C. Stamnes, "Development and Application of a Model of Self-Efficacy: Implications for Understanding Academic Success and Failure" (Ph. D. diss., University of California, Santa Barbara, 1987).

2. W. Ryan, *Blaming the Victim* (New York: Vintage Books, 1971).

3. D. Radcliff, "The Underclass Myth" (Letter to the editor), *The Progressive* 55 (December 1991): 6.

4. A. D. Hammonds, "The Black Underclass: Conflicting Perspectives," *The Western Journal of Black Studies* 13 (Winter 1989): 217–222.

5. M. Parenti, *Power and the Powerless* (New York: St. Martin's Press, 1978), 24.

6. Ibid.

CHAPTER 1. ACADEMIC ACHIEVEMENT

1. H. Kohl, *36 Children* (New York: The New American Library, 1967).

2. J. R. Mingle, *Focus on Minorities: Trends in Higher Education Participation and Success* (Denver: Education Commission of the States and State Higher Education Executive Officers, 1987).

3. J. Kozol, *Illiterate America* (Garden City, NY: Doubleday, 1985).

4. C. R. Wharton, "'Demanding Families' and Black Achievement," *Education Week* (1986): 24.

5. J. A. Mirman, R. J. Swartz, and J. Barett, "Strategies to Help Teachers Empower At-Risk Students," in *At-Risk Students and Thinking: Perspectives from Research*, ed. B. Z. Presseisen (Washington, D. C.: National Education Association and Research for Better Schools, 1988), 138–156.

6. C. Jencks, *Inequality: A Reassessment of the Effect of Family and Schooling in America* (New York: Basic Books, 1972).

7. S. McLanahan and L. Bumpass, "Comment: A Note on the Effect of Family Structure on School Enrollment," in *Divided Opportunities: Minorities, Poverty, and Social Policy*, ed. G. D. Sandefur and M. Tienda (New York: Plenum Press, 1988), 195–203.

8. Ibid.

9. T. Muller and T. J. Espenshade, *The Fourth Wave: California's Newest Immigrants* (Washington, D. C.: The Urban Institute Press, 1985).

10. Wharton, 24.

11. R. Clark, *Family Life and School Achievement: Why Poor Black Children Succeed or Fail* (Chicago: University of Chicago Press, 1983).

12. Los Angeles County and City Human Relations Commission, *McCone Revisited: A Focus on Solutions to Continuing Problems in South Central Los Angeles* (Los Angeles: Author, January, 1985; ERIC Document Reproduction Service No. ED 267 141).

13. Jencks.

14. Ibid.

15. Jonathan Kozol's book *Savage Inequalities: Children in America's Schools* (New York: Crown Publishers, 1991) offers a compelling look at the education of the poor in the United States. He includes a clear explanation of educational funding which graphically depicts the inequities in the public education system.

16. Clark, 211.

17. A. G. Powell, E. Farrar, and D. K. Cohen, *The Shopping Mall High School: Winners and Losers in the Educational Marketplace* (Boston: Houghton Mifflin, 1985).

18. R. C. Rist, "Student Social Class and Teacher Expectations: The Self-Fulfilling Prophecy in Ghetto Education," *Harvard Educational Review* 40:411–451.

19. R. C. Rist, *The Urban School: A Factory for Failure* (Cambridge, MA: MIT Press, 1973).

20. Ibid., 212.

21. Ibid., 237.

22. Powell et al.

23. Mingle.

24. Ibid.

25. Ibid.

26. "California Assessment Program Test Scores," *Los Angeles Times*, (12 June, 1988): sec. II, 2.

27. Mingle.

28. "President of ACE Seeks End to Use of Standardized Tests in Admissions," *The Chronicle of Higher Education* 34 (November 25, 1987): A32.

29. S. Jaschik, "Major Changes Seen Needed for Colleges to Attract Minorities," *The Chronicle of Higher Education* 34 (November 25, 1987): 1, A31–A32.

30. Mingle.

31. Carnegie Forum on Education and the Economy's Task Force on Teaching as a Profession, *A Nation Prepared: Teachers for the 21st Century* (New York: Carnegie Corporation, 1986).

32. Jaschik.

33. R. Solomon and J. Solomon, *Up the University: Re-creating Higher Education in America* (Reading, MA: Addison-Wesley, 1993), 85.

34. Mingle.

35. Ibid.

36. Jaschik.

37. M. Harrington, *The Other America* (London: Penguin Books, 1962).

CHAPTER 2. FAMILIES IN WATTS

1. A. Mirande, *The Chicano Experience* (Notre Dame: University of Notre Dame Press, 1985).

2. E. W. Read, "Birth Cycle," *The Wall Street Journal* 117 (March 17, 1988): 1, 13.

3. W. J. Wilson, *The Truly Disadvantaged* (Chicago: University of Chicago Press, 1987).

4. H. R. Rodgers, *Poor Women, Poor Families* (Armonk, NY: M. E. Sharpe, 1986).

5. Ibid.

6. B. Roscoe and T. S. Kruger, "AIDS: Late Adolescents' Knowledge and Its Influence on Sexual Behavior," *Adolescence* 25 (Spring, 1990): 39–47.

7. Read.

8. L. Dash, "When Children Want Children," *Society* 27 (July/August, 1990): 17–19.

9. A. Trotter, "Exposing the Drug Trade's Evil Face," *The American School Board Journal* 177 (August, 1990): 25–28, 31.

10. B. Flanigan, A. McLean, C. Hall, and V. Propp, "Alcohol Use as a Situational Influence on Young Women's Pregnancy Risk-taking Behaviors," *Adolescence* 25 (Spring, 1990): 205–214.

11. J. M. Pete and L. DeSantis, "Sexual Decision Making in Young Black Adolescent Females," *Adolescence* 25 (Spring, 1990): 145–154.

12. C. D. Hayes, ed., *Risking the Future* (Washington, DC: National Academy Press, 1987).

13. Ibid.

14. Rodgers.

15. Wilson.

16. Ibid.

17. S. B. Kamerman, "Young, Poor, and a Mother Alone: Problems and Possible Solutions," in *Services to Young Families*, ed. H. McAdoo and T. M. J. Parham (Washington, DC: American Public Welfare Association, 1985), 1–38.

and T. M. J. Parham (Washington, DC: American Public Welfare Association, 1985), 1–38.

18. S. McLanahan and L. Bumpass, "Comment: A Note on the Effect of Family Structure on School Enrollment," in *Divided Opportunities: Minorities, Poverty, and Social Policy*, ed. G. D. Sandefur and M. Tienda (New York: Plenum Press, 1988), 195–203.

19. Flanigan et al.

20. H. K. D. Singh, "Stork Reality: Why America's Infants Are Dying," *Policy Review* 52 (Spring, 1990): 56–63.

21. Hayes.

22. I. Garfinkle and S. S. McLanahan, *Single Mothers and Their Children* (Washington, DC: The Urban Institute Press, 1986).

23. R. Daniels, "Confronting the 'State of Emergency'," *Z Magazine* (June, 1993): 15–18.

24. M. Parenti, *Power and the Powerless* (New York: St. Martin's Press, 1978), 67.

25. National Center for Health Statistics, "Advance Report of Final Mortality Statistics, 1980," *Monthly Vital Statistics Report* 32 (1983).

26. H. McAdoo, "Foreword: Preventing Dependency," in *Services to Young Families*, ed. H. McAdoo and T. M. J. Parham (Washington, DC: American Public Welfare Association, 1985), VI–XVII.

27. Rodgers.

28. D. Bakan, *Slaughter of the Innocents* (San Francisco: Jossey-Bass, 1971).

29. S. Carter, "Children of Crisis," *Z Magazine* 4 (January, 1991): 33–36.

30. C. Greenland, *Preventing CAN Deaths* (London: Tavistock Publications, 1987).

31. S. M. Smith, *The Battered Child Syndrome* (London: Butterworths, 1976).

32. Y. Channer and N. Parton, "Racism, Cultural Relativism and Child Protection," in *Taking Child Abuse Seriously*, ed. The Violence against Children Study Group (London: Unwin Hyman, 1990), 107–120.

33. J. Hearn, "'Child Abuse' and Men's Violence," in *Taking Child Abuse Seriously*, ed. The Violence against Children Study Group (London: Unwin Hyman, 1990), 63–85.

34. M. D. Pagelow, *Family Violence* (New York: Praeger Publishers, 1984).

35. Ibid.

36. Smith.

37. Greenland.

38. J. Kaufman and E. Zigler, "The Intergenerational Transmission of Child Abuse," in *Child Maltreatment*, ed. D. Cicchetti and V. Carlson (Cambridge: Cambridge University Press, 1989), 129–150.

39. Pagelow.

40. Ibid.

41. Nathaniel Hawthorne, *The Scarlet Letter* (New York: Aire-mont Publishing, 1962).

42. Pagelow, 179.

CHAPTER 3. GANGS

1. J. S. Stumphauzer, E. V. Veloz, and T. W. Aiken, "Violence by Street Gangs: East Side Story?" in *Violent Behavior: Social Learning Approaches to Prediction, Management and Treatment,* ed. R. B. Stuart (New York: Brunner/Mazel, 1981), 68–82.

2. Ibid.

3. L. Bing, "Confessions from the Crossfire," *L. A. Weekly* 10 (May 6–12, 1988): 22–24, 26, 140.

4. L. Bing, "When You're a Crip (or a Blood)," *Harper's Magazine* 278 (March, 1989): 51–59.

5. "Youth and Violence: The Current Crisis," Hearing before the Select Committee on Children, Youth, and Families. House of Representatives, 100th Congress, 2nd session. Congress of the United States, Washington, DC (March 9, 1988; ERIC Document Reproduction Service No. ED 299 526).

6. R. Daniels, "Confronting the 'State of Emergency,'" *Z Magazine* 6 (June, 1993): 16.

7. "Youth and Violence."

8. D. O. Lewis, C. Mallouh, and V. Webb, "Child Abuse, Delinquency, and Violent Criminality," in *Child Maltreatment,* ed. D. Cicchetti and V. Carlson (Cambridge: Cambridge University Press, 1989), 707–721.

9. Ibid.

10. Ibid.

11. Stumphauzer et al.

12. Ramsey Clark, "A Few Modest Proposals to Reduce Individual Violence in America," in *Violence and the Violent Individual,* ed. J. R. Harys, T. K. Roberts, and K. S. Solway (New York: SP Medical and Scientific Books, 1981), 1–5.

13. Bing, 1989, p. 53.

14. Ibid.

15. "Youth and Violence."

16. Stumphauzer et al.

17. Bing, 1988.

18. C. J. L. Murray, "Mortality Among Black Men," *The New England Journal of Medicine* 322 (January 18, 1991): 205–206.

19. "Youth and Violence."
20. Clark, 4.

CHAPTER 4. SUBSTANCE ABUSE

1. S. Cohen, *The Substance Abuse Problems* (New York: Haworth Press, 1981).
2. A. Diver, "Adolescence," *International Encyclopedia of Education*, Vol. 1. (Oxford: Pergamon Press, 1985).
3. B. A. Christiansen, M. S. Goldman, and A. Inn, "Development of Alcohol-related Expectancies in Adolescents: Separating Pharmacological from Social-Learning Influences," *Journal of Consulting and Clinical Psychology* 50 (June, 1982): 336–344.
4. Ibid.
5. D. B. Kandel, "Parenting Styles, Drug Use, and Children's Adjustment in Families of Young Adults," *Journal of Marriage and the Family* 52 (February, 1990): 183–196.
6. W. D. Watts and L. S. Wright, "The Relationship of Alcohol, Tobacco, Marijuana, and Other Illegal Drug Use to Delinquency among Mexican-American, Black, and White Adolescent Males," *Adolescence* 25 (Spring, 1990): 171–181.
7. Cohen.
8. O. Amuleru-Marshall, "Substance Abuse among America's Urban Youth," *The Urban League Review* 13 (Summer/Winter, 1989–90): 93–98.
9. A. Trotter, "Exposing the Drug Trade's Evil Face," *The American School Board Journal* 177 (August, 1990): 25–28, 31.

CHAPTER 5. STRESS, EDUCATION,
AND THE INNER CITY

1. Los Angeles County and City Human Relations Commission, *McCone Revisited: A Focus on Solutions to Continuing Problems in South Central Los Angeles* (Los Angeles: Author, January, 1985; ERIC Document Reproduction Service No. ED 267 141).
2. Ibid.
3. L. Timnick, "Children of Violence," *Los Angeles Times Magazine* (September 3, 1989): 6–15.
4. Ibid.
5. I. L. Livingston and R. J. Marshall, "Cardiac Reactivity and Elevated Blood Pressure Levels among Young African Americans: The Importance of Stress," *The Urban League Review* 13 (Summer/Winter, 1989–90): 77–91.

6. B. C. Myers, "Hypertension as a Manifestation of the Stress Experienced by Black Families," in *Black Families*, ed. H. E. Cheatham and J. B. Stewart (New Brunswick, NJ: Transaction Publishers, 1990), 199–216.

7. Ibid.

8. Ibid.

9. W. B. Harvey, P. F. Bitting, and T. L. Robinson, "Between a Rock and a Hard Place: Drugs and Schools in African American Communities," *The Urban League Review* 13 (Summer/Winter, 1989–90): 113–128.

10. A. C. Diver-Stamnes, "Assessing the Effectiveness of an Inner-city High School Peer Counseling Program," *Urban Education* 26 (October, 1991): 269–284.

CHAPTER 6. IN THE WAKE OF THE UPRISING

1. S. Stolberg, "Jurors Felt King's Actions Were To Blame," *Los Angeles Times* (April 30, 1992): 1, 23.

2. V. Kotowitz, "The Death and Destruction Spread," *Los Angeles Times* (May 11, 1992): T12.

3. "Everybody is Pointin' Their Finger at Everybody," *Los Angeles Times* (May 13, 1992): T7.

4. Kotowitz.

5. R. Takaki, *Strangers from a Different Shore* (New York: Penguin Books, 1989).

6. "The Path to Fury," *Los Angeles Times* (May 11, 1992): T10.

7. "Everybody Is Pointin'," T7.

8. "Everybody Was Going In," *Los Angeles Times* (May 13, 1992): T5.

9. "I Took the Beds," *Los Angeles Times* (May 13, 1992): T4.

10. National Advisory Commission on Civil Disorders, *Report of the National Advisory Commission on Civil Disorders* (New York: Bantam Books, 1968).

11. "New Faces in the Neighborhood," *Los Angeles Times* (May 11, 1992): T9.

12. "These Problems Aren't about Race; They're about Class," *Los Angeles Times* (May 13, 1992): T11.

13. "When They Were Looting the Store, I Was Just Laughing," *Los Angeles Times* (May 13, 1992): T10.

CHAPTER 7. SUGGESTIONS FOR CHANGE

1. H. K. D. Singh, "Stork Reality: Why America's Infants are Dying," *Policy Review* 52 (Spring, 1990): 56–63.

2. H. R. Rodgers, *Poor Women, Poor Families* (Armonk, NY: M. E. Sharpe, 1986).

3. Singh.

4. Ibid.

5. C. Marks, "Occasional Laborers and Chronic Want: A Review of *The Truly Disadvantaged*," *Journal of Sociology and Social Welfare* 16 (December, 1989): 57–68.

6. C. T. Ramey and S. L. Ramey, "Intensive Educational Intervention for Children of Poverty," *Intelligence* 14 (1990): 1–9.

7. W. Johnson, "President's Perspective," *United Teacher* 20 (May 12, 1989): 2.

8. D. U. Levine, "Educating Alienated Inner-City Youth: Lessons from Street Academies," Author (November, 1972; ERIC Document Reproduction Service No. ED 090 326).

9. J. Kozol, *Illiterate America* (Garden City, NY: Doubleday, 1985).

10. P. Dreir, "Bush to Cities: Drop Dead," *The Progressive* 56 (July, 1992): 20–23.

11. Ibid.

12. R. Holland, director and producer, *The Fire This Time* (Los Angeles, Blacktop Films), 1994. This is a powerful documentary sketching the history of African American oppression in southern California and exploring the causes of the 1992 civil unrest. It uses the voices of people in the community to explore difficult issues of racism, prejudice, disenfranchisement, and oppression.

13. Los Angeles County Commission on Human Relations, *Minority Youth Unemployment: Barriers to Success in the Labor Market* (Los Angeles: Author, September, 1985; ERIC Document Reproduction Service No. ED 267 142).

14. M. Harrington, *The Other America* (London: Penguin Books, 1962), 171.

REFERENCES

Amuleru-Marshall, O. (1989–90, Summer/Winter). Substance abuse among America's urban youth. *The Urban League Review, 13,* 1–2, pp. 93–98.

Bakan, D. (1971). *Slaughter of the innocents.* San Francisco: Jossey-Bass.

Bing, L. (1988, May 6–12). Confessions from the crossfire. *L. A. Weekly, 10,* No. 24, pp. 22–24, 26, 140.

Bing, L. (1989, March). When you're a Crip (or a Blood). *Harper's Magazine, 278,* 1666, pp. 51–59.

California Assessment Program test scores. (1988, June 12). *Los Angeles Times,* Part II, p. 2.

Carnegie Forum on Education and the Economy's Task Force on Teaching as a Profession. (1986). *A Nation Prepared: Teachers for the 21st Century.* New York: Carnegie Corporation.

Carter, S. (1991, January). Children of crisis. *Z Magazine, 4,* 1, pp. 33–36.

Channer, Y., and Parton, N. (1990). Racism, cultural relativism and child protection. In The Violence against Children Study Group (Eds.), *Taking Child Abuse Seriously* (pp. 107–120). London: Unwin Hyman.

Christiansen, B. A., Goldman, M. S., and Inn, A. (1982, June). Development of alcohol-related expectancies in adolescents: Separating pharmacological from social-learning influences. *Journal of Consulting and Clinical Psychology, 50,* 3, pp. 336–344.

Clark, R. (1981). A few modest proposals to reduce individual violence in America. In J. R. Harys, T. K. Roberts, and K. S. Solway (Eds.), *Violence and the Violent Individual* (pp. 1–5). New York: SP Medical and Scientific Books.

Clark, R. (1983). *Family life and school achievement: Why poor black children succeed or fail.* Chicago: University of Chicago Press.

Cohen, S. (1981). *The substance abuse problems.* New York: Haworth Press.

Daniels, R. (1993, June). Confronting the "state of emergency," *Z Magazine, 6,* 6, pp. 15–18.

Dash, L. (1990, July/August). When children want children. *Society, 27,* 5, pp. 17–19.

Diver, A. (1985). Adolescence. *International Encyclopedia of Education,* Vol. 1. Oxford: Pergamon Press.

Diver-Stamnes, A. C. (1991, October). Assessing the effectiveness of an inner-city high school peer counseling program. *Urban Education, 26,* 3, 269–284.

Dreir, P. (1992, July). Bush to cities: Drop dead. *The Progressive, 56,* 7, 20–23.

Edelman, M. W. (1987). *Families in peril.* Cambridge: Harvard University Press.

Everybody is pointin' their finger at everybody. (1992, May 13). *Los Angeles Times,* p. T7.

Everybody was going in. (1992, May 13). *Los Angeles Times,* p. T5.

Flanigan, B., McLean, A., Hall, C., and Propp, V. (1990, Spring). Alcohol use as a situational influence on young women's pregnancy risk-taking behaviors. *Adolescence, 25,* 97, pp. 205–214.

Garfinkle, I., and McLanahan, S. S. (1986). *Single mothers and their children.* Washington, DC: The Urban Institute Press.

Greenland, C. (1987). *Preventing CAN deaths.* London: Tavistock Publications.

Hammonds, A. D. (1989, Winter). The black underclass: Conflicting perspectives. *The Western Journal of Black Studies, 13,* 4, pp. 217–222.

Harrington, M. (1962). *The other America.* London: Penguin Books.

Harvey, W. B., Bitting, P. F., and Robinson, T. L. (1989–90, Summer/Winter). Between a rock and a hard place: Drugs and schools in African American communities. *The Urban League Review, 13,* 1–2, pp. 113–128.

Hawthorne, N. (1962). *The scarlet letter.* New York: Airmont Publishing.

Hayes, C. D. (Ed.) (1987). *Risking the future.* Washington, DC: National Academy Press.

Hearn, J. (1990). "Child abuse" and men's violence. In The Violence against Children Study Group (Eds.), *Taking Child Abuse Seriously* (pp. 63–85). London: Unwin Hyman.

Holland, R. (Producer and director). (1994). *The fire this time* (Film). Los Angeles: Blacktop Films.

I took the beds. (1992, May 13). *Los Angeles Times,* p. T4.

Jaschik, S. (1987, November 25). Major changes seen needed for colleges to attract minorities. *The Chronicle of Higher Education, 34,* pp. 1, A31-A32.

Jencks, C. (1972). *Inequality: A reassessment of the effect of family and schooling in America.* New York: Basic Books.

Johnson, W. (1989, May 12). President's perspective. *United Teacher, 20,* 16, p. 2.

Kamerman, S. B. (1985). Young, poor, and a mother alone: Problems and possible solutions. In H. McAdoo and T. M. J. Parham (Eds.),

Services to Young Families (pp. 1–38). Washington, DC: American Public Welfare Association.

Kandel, D. B. (1990, February). Parenting styles, drug use, and children's adjustment in families of young adults. *Journal of Marriage and the Family, 52*, 1, pp. 183–196.

Kaufman, J., and Zigler, E. (1989). The intergenerational transmission of child abuse. In D. Cicchetti and V. Carlson (Eds.), *Child Maltreatment* (pp. 129–150). Cambridge: Cambridge University Press.

Kohl, H. (1967). *36 children.* New York: The New American Library.

Kotowitz, V. (1992, May 11). The death and destruction spread. *Los Angeles Times*, p. T12.

Kozol, J. (1985). *Illiterate America.* Garden City, NY: Doubleday.

Kozol, J. (1991). *Savage inequalities: Children in America's schools.* New York: Crown Publishers.

Levine, D. U. (1972, November). Educating alienated inner-city youth: Lessons from street academies. Author. (ERIC Document Reproduction Service No. ED 090 326.)

Lewis, D. O., Mallouh, C., and Webb, V. (1989). Child abuse, delinquency, and violent criminality. In D. Cicchetti and V. Carlson (Eds.), *Child Maltreatment* (pp. 707–721). Cambridge: Cambridge University Press.

Livingston, I. L., and Marshall, R. J. (1989–90, Summer/Winter). Cardiac reactivity and elevated blood pressure levels among young African Americans: The importance of stress. *The Urban League Review, 13*, 1–2, pp. 77–91.

Los Angeles County and City Human Relations Commission. (1985, January). *McCone revisited: A focus on solutions to continuing problems in South Central Los Angeles.* Los Angeles: Author. (ERIC Document Reproduction Service No. ED 267 141.)

Los Angeles County Commission on Human Relations. (1985, September). *Minority youth unemployment: Barriers to success in the labor market.* Los Angeles: Author. (ERIC Document Reproduction Service No. ED 267 142.)

Marks, C. (1989, December). Occasional laborers and chronic want: A review of *The Truly Disadvantaged. Journal of Sociology and Social Welfare, 16*, 4, pp. 57–68.

Martinex-Schnell, B., and Waxweiler, R. J. (1989). Increases in premature mortality due to homicide: United States, 1968–1985. *Violence and Victims, 4*, 4, pp. 287–293.

McAdoo, H. (1985). Foreword: Preventing dependency. In H. McAdoo and T. M. J. Parham (Eds.) *Services to Young Families* (pp. VI–XVII). Washington, DC: American Public Welfare Association.

McCord, C., and Freeman, H. (1990). Excess mortality in Harlem. *New England Journal of Medicine, 322*, 3, pp. 173–177.

McLanahan, S., and Bumpass, L. (1988). Comment: A note on the effect of family structure on school enrollment. In G. D. Sandefur and M. Tienda (Eds.), *Divided Opportunities: Minorities, Poverty, and Social Policy* (pp. 195–203). New York: Plenum Press.

McLanahan, S., Garfinkel, I., and Watson, D. (1988). Family structure, poverty, and the underclass. In M. G. H. McGeary and L. E. Lynn, Jr. (Eds.), *Urban Change and Poverty* (pp. 102–147). Washington, DC: National Academy Press.

Mingle, J. R. (1987). *Focus on minorities: Trends in higher education participation and success.* Denver: Education Commission of the States and State Higher Education Executive Officers.

Mirande, A. (1985). *The Chicano experience.* Notre Dame: University of Notre Dame Press.

Mirman, J. A., Swartz, R. J., and Barett, J. (1988). Strategies to help teachers empower at-risk students. In B. Z. Presseisen (Ed.), *At-Risk Students and Thinking: Perspectives from Research* (pp. 138–156). Washington, DC: National Education Association and Research for Better Schools.

Muller, T. and Espenshade, T. J. (1985). *The fourth wave: California's newest immigrants.* Washington, DC: The Urban Institute Press.

Murray, C. J. L. (1991, January 18). Mortality among Black Men. *The New England Journal of Medicine, 322,* 3, pp. 205–206.

Myers, B. C. (1990). Hypertension as a manifestation of the stress experienced by black families. In H. E. Cheatham and J. B. Stewart (Eds.), *Black Families* (pp. 199–216). New Brunswick, NJ: Transaction Publishers.

National Advisory Commission on Civil Disorders. (1968). *Report of the National Advisory Commission on Civil Disorders.* New York: Bantam Books.

National Center for Health Statistics. (1983). Advance report of final mortality statistics, 1980. *Monthly Vital Statistics Report, 32,* 4.

New faces in the neighborhood. (1992, May 11). *Los Angeles Times,* p. T9.

Pagelow, M. D. (1984). *Family violence.* New York: Praeger Publishers.

Parenti, M. (1978). *Power and the powerless.* New York: St. Martin's Press.

Path to Fury. (1992, May 11). The path to fury. *Los Angeles Times,* p. T10.

Pete, J. M., and DeSantis, L. (1990, Spring). Sexual decision making in young black adolescent females. *Adolescence 25,* 97, pp. 145–154.

Powell, A. G., Farrar, E., and Cohen, D. K. (1985). *The shopping mall high school: Winners and losers in the educational marketplace.* Boston: Houghton Mifflin.

President of ACE seeks end to use of standardized tests in admissions. (1987, November 25). *The Chronicle of Higher Education, 34,* p. A32.

Radcliff, D. (1991, December). The underclass myth (Letter to the editor). *The Progressive, 55,* 12, p. 6.

Ramey, C. T., and Ramey, S. L. (1990). Intensive educational intervention for children of poverty. *Intelligence, 14,* 1, pp. 1–9.

Read, E. W. (1988, March 17). Birth cycle. *The Wall Street Journal, 117,* 53, pp. 1, 13.

Rist, R. C. (1970). Student social class and teacher expectations: The self-fulfilling prophecy in ghetto education. *Harvard Educational Review, 40,* 411–451.

Rist, R. C. (1973). *The urban school: A factory for failure.* Cambridge, MA: MIT Press.

Rodgers, H. R. (1986). *Poor women, poor families.* Armonk, NY: M. E. Sharpe.

Roscoe, B., and Kruger, T. S. (1990, Spring). AIDS: Late adolescents' knowledge and its influence on sexual behavior. *Adolescence, 25, 97,* pp. 39–47.

Ryan, W. (1971.) *Blaming the victim.* New York: Vintage Books.

Sawhill, I. V. (1989, Summer). The underclass: 1—An overview. *The Public Interest, 96,* pp. 3–15.

Shapiro, A. L. (1991, April 29). We're no. 1! We're no. 1! *The Nation, 252,* 16, p. 544.

Singh, H. K. D. (1990, Spring). Stork reality: Why America's infants are dying. *Policy Review, 52,* pp. 56–63.

Smith, S. M. (1976). *The battered child syndrome.* London: Butterworths.

Solomon, R., and Solomon, J. (1993). *Up the university: Re-creating higher education in America.* Reading, MA: Addison-Wesley.

Stamnes, A. C. (1987). *Development and application of a model of self-efficacy: Implications for understanding academic success and failure* (Ph. D. diss., University of California, Santa Barbara).

Stolberg, S. (1992, April 30). Jurors felt King's actions were to blame. *Los Angeles Times,* pp. 1, 23.

Stumphauzer, J. S., Veloz, E. V., and Aiken, T. W. (1981). Violence by street gangs: East side story? In R. B. Stuart (Ed.), *Violent Behavior: Social Learning Approaches to Prediction, Management and Treatment* (pp. 68–82). New York: Brunner/Mazel.

Takaki, R. (1989). *Strangers from a different shore.* New York: Penguin Books.

These problems aren't about race; they're about class. (1992, May 13). *Los Angeles Times,* p. T11.

Timnick, L. (1989, September 3). Children of violence. *Los Angeles Times Magazine,* pp. 6–15.

Trotter, A. (1990, August). Exposing the drug trade's evil face. *The American School Board Journal, 177,* 8, pp. 25–28, 31.

Watts, W. D., and Wright, L. S. (1990, Spring). The relationship of alcohol, tobacco, marijuana, and other illegal drug use to delinquency among Mexican-American, black, and white adolescent males. *Adolescence*, 25, 97, pp. 171–181.

Wharton, C. R. (1986). 'Demanding families' and black achievement. *Education Week*, 24.

When they were looting the store, I was just laughing. (1992, May 13). *Los Angeles Times*, p. T10.

Williams, M. W. (1990). Polygamy and the declining male to female ratio in black communities: A social inquiry. In H. E. Cheatham and J. B. Stewart (Eds.) *Black Families* (pp. 171–193). New Brunswick: Transaction Publishers.

Wilson, W. J. (1987). *The truly disadvantaged*. Chicago: University of Chicago Press.

Youth and Violence: The Current Crisis. (March 9, 1988). Hearing before the Select Committee on Children, Youth, and Families. House of Representatives, 100th Congress, 2nd session. Congress of the United States, Washington, DC. (ERIC Document Reproduction Service No. ED 299 526.)

INDEX